Oswald Cockayne

Seinte Marherete the meiden ant martyr, in Old English

First edited from the skin books in 1862

Oswald Cockayne

Seinte Marherete the meiden ant martyr, in Old English
First edited from the skin books in 1862

ISBN/EAN: 9783741195730

Manufactured in Europe, USA, Canada, Australia, Japa

Cover: Foto ©Andreas Hilbeck / pixelio.de

Manufactured and distributed by brebook publishing software (www.brebook.com)

Oswald Cockayne

Seinte Marherete the meiden ant martyr, in Old English

Seinte Marherete

The Meiden ant Martyr,

IN OLD ENGLISH.

FIRST EDITED FROM THE SKIN BOOKS IN 1862,

BY

OSWALD COCKAYNE, M.A.,
FORMERLY OF ST. JOHNS COLLEGE, CAMBRIDGE,

AND NOW REISSUED.

LONDON:
PUBLISHED FOR THE EARLY ENGLISH TEXT SOCIETY,
BY TRÜBNER & CO., 60, PATERNOSTER ROW.

MDCCCLXVI.
Price Two Shillings.

LONDON:
Printed by TAYLOR & FRANCIS, Red Lion Court, Fleet Street.

REVIEW.

The following remarks are þe result of þe criticism which an editor passes upon his own former efforts, chastised occasionally by friendly or angry suggestions from wiþout.

Since the "Foreword" was written, Mr. James Morton, who by his publications of þe "Ancren Riwle" and "St. Catherine" deserved well of students of our old language, is deceased. Were it possible to recall any sharp expression about his scholarship, it should be done. His services were far greater þan his shortcomings. Prebendary of Lincoln, Vicar of Holbeach, and Chaplain to Earl Grey, he seems to have enjoyed the respect of all around him. EJVS ANIMÆ PROPITIETVR DEVS.

P. viii. It has been more plainly said by a gentleman cognisant of þe facts, þat þe Trinity MS. is "not forðcoming:" þe more widely þis is known, þe better; for it gives more hope of restoration to þe owners.

Mr. Beriah Botfields catalogue of the Durham Library contains, at p. 155, the story of St. Margarete in verse, by John Lidgate. A black letter edition, wiþout date, of the "Lyfe of Saynt Marguret," printed by John Mitchell, I have not seen, except in a sale catalogue.

P. 98. Cost. Add "gecostan cempan." Cod. Exon. p. 107, l. 21.

P. 99. Cornuc, *orane*, is found in an unpublished glossary.

P. 101. Ende, Ande, masc. plural; andas occurs in not a few passages: one of þe best is in the glossary of Moyen Moutier, "Tempe, sceaduge andas;" that is, $T\acute{\epsilon}\mu\pi\eta$, *shadowy districts*, which is an unexceptionable translation.

Farlac. What occurs fol. 44. a. 17 is not an example of Farlac, *fear*. For it may be substituted þe quotation on p. 100, under Duuelunge, and þere "ba" is correctly given from both print and MS. Mennissclegge, Modeglegge should have been printed.

On p. 102 Hendeleic is the MS. spelling. Wouleche is printed by Mr. Morton; but Na wohlac nif fe culuert is found in MS. Cott. Titus D. xvii. 27. d. Reflac (not Replac), Ancren R. fol. 53. b. 54. b.

P. 106. Melseocel. I recall þe epiðet "hibrid." See Surmelsc in Leechdoms.

P. 108. Steap. Add Steap, *brilliant*, Sol. and Sat. p. 161, line 750, p. 170, line 827.

P. 109. Stew. Add from Coventry Mysteries, p. 217:
Stow that harlot some erthely wyght
That in advowtyre here is ffownde.

P. 112. Wedlac. Read Matth. i. 18.

CONTENTS.

	Page
SEINTE MARHERETE a text of 1200	1
SEINTE MARGARETE a text of 1330	24
MEIDAN MAREGRETE from Hickes	34
Various Readings and Notes	44
SEINTE MARHERETE Modernized	51
On the Language of S. MARHERETE	74
Glossary..	97

FOREWORD.

The little book now laid before the few, who turn their eyes lovingly upon the history and records of their own language, aims at being a critical edition of the short piece, which stands first in order of time; partly to show that the English of the twelfth and thirteenth centuries is not a mere corruption and contemptible, and partly because the critical study of the Greek and Latin authors gives the mind a bias to a like treatment of the English.

The text according to the true theory of a critical edition should have been made as perfect as possible, whether by collation or emendation. But the present generation of English scholars has not advanced to that point. They expect an adherence to the manuscript, and will condemn deviations from it. Yielding therefore to circumstances I have rarely altered the text of MS. R., and when I have so done, it has been on the authority of MS. B. Suggestions for improvement of the text so resulting will be found in the notes.

An alliterative text should, many will pronounce, have been printed in short verses, as poetry. The manuscripts, however, write straight away from end to end of the ruled lines, and this was done in the earlier times, as in the original copy of Cædmon. To abide by the example of our forefathers in printing their compositions seemed most fair and proper. The only advantage of the other course is to bring out the versification more distinctly. To do that would in a few instances have led to a constraint upon my conviction, that the writer has in some instances come very near to prose. Sir F. Madden in turning Layamon from the skinbook shape to the broken verses of the printed edition has considered the sign ⁊ to be wholly metrical, as perhaps in the fourteenth century it often was. He says (vol. iii. p. 440), "It may here be as well to state, that in commencing the work, the editor proposed to follow the punctuation of the MS. in every case, but on proceeding further the errors of the scribe became so frequent and so obvious in this respect, that it was resolved to adopt an uniform punctuation throughout, of half pause and full pause." Mr. Hardwick made the same complaint: "The dots or points by which Anglo-Saxon verse is mainly distinguishable, have disappeared or been misplaced through the negligence of the scribes; on which account as well as for greater distinctness, the sentences are now broken into their subordinate clauses, by the use of modern punctuation " (St. Cath. p. 21.) My remarks upon this matter will concern only the piece I have printed; I do not criticise either of these gentlemen: it has been my wish to print everything as I found it as much as might be, and more than in all cases seemed best; yet the stop ⁊ was not purely metrical, it in early times indicated a pause in the sense, and is found in prose; thus it appears in a landboc of Eadweard in 1045 A.D. (cod. dipl. dcclxxxi.) It is also found in Domesday Book about 1085 A.D. In one place of St. Marherete it is evidently (fol. 41. a. 15) intended to point out that the writer desired to read the adverb ʒeomerliche with the verb ʒerdede and not with ʒeide.

The alliteration used is not of that elaborate kind of which Conybeare, Rask and others have treated, and on which they have quarrelled, but of that easy negligent sort which seemed good enough when the battle lay of Brunanburh was written: it pleases the ear and is never allowed to interfere with the sense or the poetic diction, unless Rondin (fol. 42. a. 3) be somewhat forced.

The volume MS. Reg. 17. A. xxvii. is a small quarto on vellum transcribed, if I rightly quote Sir F. Madden, about A.D. 1230. It contains a fanciful piece on the text, Si sciret paterfamilias (fol. 1 to 11. b.); the lives of St. Catherine (fol. 11. b. to 37), St. Marherete, St. Juliana (fol. 56. to 70. b.), and ends with a leaf of the Oreisun of St. Mary, imperfect. At the end of the first piece are the following words, Par feínte charité biddeð a pater nost' for iohan þat þeof boc wrat; which doubtless convey only the name of the scribe. The Bodleian MS. is described as beginning on the first leaf with a rubricated title, which is almost entirely obliterated; then begins the text of St. Catherine, " Costentin ant Maxence," and then St. Margaret. The collation of this MS. was forwarded to me from Oxford, and I have had no opportunity of seeing the volume.

Sir F. Madden (Layamon, vol. iii. p. 350) has stated that the piece was probably composed about 1200 A.D., and as it seems in some respects a few years older than the printed earlier text of Layamon, it will be as well to acquiesce in that opinion. Sir Frederic is well able to maintain any opinion he forms: but if compared with the text of the last entries in the Chronicle, written soon after 1154 and before 1177, the language of St. Marherete might be put thirty or forty years earlier. All deductions from the mode of forming characters, and often even from the inflexions and phrases, furnish only the downward limit; for transcribers altered their originals.

Several Latin equivalents of this legend are to be found; among these attention may be specially directed to MS. Harl. 5327 a small volume backed as of the eleventh century, and to MS. Harl. 2801 lettered as of the thirteenth. An earlier English equivalent, the date of which I dare not too closely determine, has been printed by me in Narratiunculæ. That the present tale did not proceed from the Saxon English is evident by comparing hpuɼuɼ (fol. 73. b. 1) with Ruffin (fol. 47. b. 11) and lımeɼ ɼeolð (fol. 74. b. 5) with Caplimet (fol. 53. a. 5). The Latin (2801) has in the last place decapoli et armenia ciuitate (fol. 64. d.).

It was of no consequence whatever to fix on the Latin from which the tale is taken. The wooing scene between "a clean man and a clean woman" occurs in no other version of the legend that I have seen, and it shows that the English maker was a proficient in his art.

The contractions of the bookfell have mostly been interpreted, there was no difficulty, and to leave them in the text would have been irksome to most readers. With that exception I have attempted to give such a facsimile of the original writing as the printers means allowed, and they have resources beyond most others. The shape of the letters, the alternations of long f and crooked s are found in the ancient copy.

St. Catherines life and martyrdom out of the same volume and by the same hand has been printed for the Abbotsford Club by the Rev. James Morton, London, 1841, but the book cannot be bought, so exclusive are the rules of that club. In the publications of the Cambridge Antiquarian Society (No. xv.) may be found, "An Historical Inquiry touching St. Catharine of Alexandria, to which is added, A Semi-Saxon Legend, by Charles Hardwick, M.A., fellow and chaplain of St. Catharine's Hall, Cambridge. 1849."

In the Glossary have been cited frequently certain pieces nearly cotemporary with the Liflade ant te passiun of Seinte Marherete. Layamon is well known from the careful editing of Sir Frederic Madden. The Ormulum edited by Dr. White is also well known. The Ancren Riwle has been printed with an interpretation for the Camden Society by the Rev. James Morton, who had previously published the Legend of St. Catherine. It will be a sufficient measure of the scholarship of this gentleman to mention, that having found Wumme, which is the reading of all three manuscripts, and being unable to interpret it, he printed Wummen and explained as Women. Wumme means Wo is me! The compositions I have called Si sciret from its first words, Hali Meidenhad from its subject, The Wooing of our Lord or Wohung of ure Louerd, from its own hint, are yet confined to the original parchments. As cotemporary pieces they were closely searched, and lent me much aid in illustrating and understanding the legend now printed.

The second poem in this collection is from an Harleian skin book containing a large number of saints lives, executed, it may be, about 1330. The histories of St. Brandan and St. Thomas Beket have been given in the volumes of the Percy Society. Several other lives are in print, and on the point of publication by another Society. The language is easily read by all who know anything of these times, and may be soon understood by a beginner with the help of one of the glossaries.

The third comes from Hickes, who obtained it from an original in the library of Trinity College, Cambridge. Hickes has made some staring blunders, and I had hoped to have corrected both these and the uncertain shapes of his letters by a reference to the codex. Circumstances, however, put an obstacle in the way.

A later text has been printed in " The Lyvys of Seyntys translated into Euglys be a Doctour of Dyuynite cleppd Osbern Bokenam Frer Austyn of the Convent of Stokelare," London, 1835. The editor considers the composition to date about 1460. Among them occurs Vita Scæ Margaretæ Virginis et Martiris. It commences thus:—

    Whylom as the story | techeth us
    In Antioche | that grit cyte
    A man ther was | clepyd Theodosius
    Wych in gret state stood | and dignyte
    For of paynymrye | the patriark was he
    And had the reule | and al the governaunce
    To whom all prestys | dede obeyance.

MS. Arundel, 327. The peculiarities were not such as seemed to deserve room here.

London, July 1862.

SEINTE MARHERETE

þE MEIDEN
ANT MARTYR.

MSS. Reg. 17. A. xxvii. Fol. 37. (R.)
MS. Bodl. 34. (B.)

feinte marherete þe meiden ant martyr. (R.)
Iþe feaderef & iþes funef & iþef hali gaftef nome, her beginneð þe liflade & te paffiun of feinte margarete. (MS. B.)

EFTER ure lauerdef pine. ant hif paffiun. ant¹² hif beð on rode. ant hif arifte of beað. ant efter hif up aftihunge af he fteh to heouene ¹⁴ peren monie martirf peopmen ba ant pummen ¹⁵ to beaðef mifliche ibon for þe nome of brihtin. ant ¹⁶ af icubd kempen ouercomen ant akaften hare þreo ¹⁷ cunne fan. þe feont ant teof pake porld. ant hare licomef luftef. ant penden of þeof peanen to peolen ¹⁹ ant to eche punnen icrunet to crifte.

²⁰ Þe ȝet peren monie ma þen nu beon mifbileuede men þe heiden ant hereden heðene ²¹ mapmez. of ftockef. ant of ftanef perkef iprahte ¹ ah ich an godef þeope theochimuf inempnet ilearet ² in godef lap. habbe ired ant araht moni mifliche leaf. ³ ant neauer in nan ftude ne mahtich underftonden ⁴ of nan þ pere purðe for to beon ipurget af hit beh ⁵ brihtin. bute þe hehe healent an þ if in heouene ⁶ þe punede hpil hif pille pef bimong porldliche men. ant ⁷ botnede blinde þe dumbe ant te deaue. ant te deade⁸ arerde to lif. ant to leomen. ant crunede hif icorne ⁹ þe beð breheð for him. oðer eni nopcin. ant alle criftene men þ beoð of crift icleopet fpa ȝef ha nutteð hare nome. haueð yenet þ lif þ echeliche ilefteð. euch ¹² ifulhet in font oþe

B

almihti feberes nome. ant oþe pitti sunes nome ant oþes hali
gastes. Þes in þe ilke time liuenbe in londe :/ þ eabi meiden
marherete bi ¹⁵ nome þ̄ faht pið þe feont. ant pið hif eorðliche
limen.¹⁶ ant ouercom ant akaste ham. ant ich bijet hit ipriten
of ¹⁷ þe pritere þa :/ al hire passiun ant hire pinful beað ¹⁸ þ
ha broh for brihtin. Þercnið alle þe mahen. ¹⁹ ant herunge
habbeð. pibepen mit te pebbebe. ant ²⁰ meibenes nomeliche
lustnin swiðe jeorne hu ²¹ ha schulen luuien þene liuienbe
lauerb ant libben ²² imerðhab þ̄ him is mihte leouest spa þ̄ ha
moten (fol. 38) þurh þe eabi meiben þ̄ pe munnið to bei pið
merðhabes² menske. þ̄ murie meibenes song singen mit tif
meiben ³ ant pið þe heoueneliche hirb echeliche in heouene.
⁴ Þis meiben þe pe munnib pes marherete ihaten. ant hire
fleschliche feber teobosie hehte of þ̄ heðene sols patriarke ant
prince. ant heo as⁷ þe beorepurðe brihtin hit bihte pes ibroht
into a ⁸ burh to seben ant to softrin from þe muchele antioche
fiftene milen. þa ha hefbe of elbe fiftene jeres. ¹⁰ ant hire
mober pes ipenb þe pei þe porlbliche men ¹¹ ane schulen ipenben.
ha parð þeo þ̄ hefbe ipist ¹² ant ipenet hire so lengre so leouere.
ant alle hire ¹³ luueben :/ þ̄ hire on lokeben as þeo þ̄ gob luuebe
þe ¹⁴ heoueneliche lauerb ant hefbe þe grace of þen hali gost ¹⁵
spa þ̄ heo ches him to luue ant to leouemon. ant bitahte in his
honb þe menske of hire merðhab to piten ¹⁷ ant to pelben
pið al hire seoluen. Þus ha pes ant piste ¹⁸ meokest an meiben
pið oðer meibenes oþe selt hire soster moberes ahte. ha
iherbe on euch half hire hu me broh to beaðe cristes icorne
for rihte bileaue. ant jirnbe ant palbe jeorne jef gobes pille
²² pere. þ̄ ha muste beon an of þe mober bern þ̄ so ¹ muche
brohen for brihtin. Bitimbe umbe stunbe þ̄ ² ter com ut of
asie toparb antioche þes feonbes ³ an softer to herien iþe hehe
burh his heðene gobes. ⁴ olibrius hehte schirreue of þ̄ lonb. þ̄
alle þeo þe lesben oþen liuienbe gobb. forbube ant forbembe. ah
as he ⁶ penbe abei his pei. he seh þeos seli meiben marherete ⁷
ant schan al of plite ant of pastum. ant het his hatterliche ⁸

neomen hire spiðe. ȝef ha if freo pummon ich hire⁹ pule habben
ant to pif halden. ȝef ha þeope if ʻ ich cheofe hire to cheuefe.
ant hire pule freom piðgerfum. ¹¹ ant pið golde. ant pel hire
fchal ipurðen for hire luffum ¹² leor ʻ pið al þ ich pelde. af
þeof cnihtef palden parpen ¹³ honden on hire. ha bigon to
cleopien ant callen þuf to crifte.
¹⁴ Þaue lauerd milce ant merci of þi pummon. ne ne ¹⁵ let
tu neauer mi faple forleofen pið þe forlorne. ¹⁶ ne pið þe luðere
mi lif þ beoð al blodi biblodeget ¹⁷ mid funne. Ihefu crift
gobef fune beo þu eauer mi ¹⁸ gleo ant mi glebunde. þe mote
ich ai mare heien. ant ¹⁹ herien. hald hehe healent min heorte
ich bifeche þe ²⁰ in treope bileaue ant bipite þu mi bodi þe if
al bitahte. from flefchliche fulðen. þ neauer mi faple ne ²¹ beo
mit funne ifulet þurh þe lichomef luft þe (fol. 39) little hpile
likeð. lauerd luft nu to me. ich habbe a ² deore ȝimftan. ant
ich hit habbe iȝeuen þe. mi meiðhab ich meane. bloftme
brihteft in bodi þe hit bereð. ⁴ ant bipit pel ne lettu neauer
þe unhpiht parpen hire ipurðinge. for hit if fpa leof þe. hit if
him þinge laðeft. he peoreð ant parpeð eauer þer toparb⁷ mid
allef cunnef prenchef. lauerd þu pere me ⁸ ant pite hit eauer to
þe. ne þole þu neauer þe ⁹ unpiht þ he peorri mi pit. ne ponie
mi pifbom. ¹⁰ ah fenb me þi fonde hehe healent of heouene.
þe ¹¹ cuðe me ant kenne hu ich onfperien fchule þif fchucke
fchirreue. for ich ifeo me lauerb biftaðeb ant ¹³ biftonben af
lomb mit peb puluef. ant af þe fuhel ¹⁴ þe if fon i þe fuheleref
grune. ant af fifch ahon on ¹⁵ hoke. af þe roa inumen iþe net.
hehe healent ¹⁶ help me nu. ne leaf þu me neauer iluðere
monne honden.
¹⁷ Þe cnihtef for ha fpec þuf cherben ¹⁸ euch an aȝein. ant
cpeðen to hare lauerb ¹⁹ ne mei þi mihte habben na man pið
þif meiben ²⁰ for ne hereð ha nane of ure heðene gobef. ah
leueð on þe lauerb þ gipef forbemben ant heðene ahongen
ant heuen on robe. Olibriuf þe luðere þa he ¹ þif iherbe.
changebe hif chere. ant beb bringen hire ² biuoren him bliue.

Sone ſo heo icumen peſ. he cleopeðe to hire þuſ. Cuð me
quoð he ȝef þu art foſter⁴ of freo monne. oðer þeop pummon.
þe eabi meiden⁵ marherete ſone him onſperebe. freo pummon
ich⁶ am ant tah gobeſ þeope. ȝe quoð he. ant hpet gobb⁷
heieſtu ant herſumeſt. ich heie qð ha gobb feber: ant hiſ⁸
beorepurðe ſune ihū criſt hatte. ant him ich habbe meiden mi
meiðhab iȝettet. ant luuie aſ leouemon ant leue ¹⁰ on aſ lauerb.
ȝe qð he lube. leueſtu ant luueſt him þe¹¹ reopðſulliche beibe
ant breorliche on robe. Yai quoð¹² heo. ah þeo þe penben
ſorto forbon him. þine forðſeberes. beoð forfarene reopliche. ant
forloren luðerliche. ant he hueð kinebern icrunet in hiſ kine-
bom¹⁵ keiſer of kingeſ echeliche in heouene. þe pari¹⁶ of þeoſ
porbeſ parð utnumen prað. ant het hire¹⁷ kaſten into cparterne.
ant into cpalmhuſ. aðet he¹⁸ heſbe betere biþoht him ohpucche
piſe he palbe¹⁹ merrin hire meiðhab. ant ferbe him ſoððen
into antioche. ant heibe hiſ heðene gobeſ. aſ hit lomp. ant lei
to hiſ²¹ luðere bileaue. het bringen hire biuoren him. ant heo
²² peſ ſone ibroht forð. ant he bigon to ſeggen. meiben (*fol.* 40)
haue merci ant milce of þe ſeoluen. nim ȝeme of þi² ȝuheðe.
ant of þi ſemli ſchape. ant of þi ſchene nebſchaſt.³ purch eſter
mi pil. ant purge mine mapmez. ant te⁴ ſchal pel ipurðen. pið
al þ ich i porlb ah. ant i palb⁵ habbe. marherete milbeſt ant
meibene meokeſt⁶ onſperebe him ant ſeibe. pite þu hit ȝef
þu pult.⁷ for he hit pat ful pel þe haueð iſeilet to him me ſeolf.
⁸ ant mi meiðhab. þ tu ne maht naneſ peiſ. pið peole⁹ ne pið
punne. pið pa ne pið ponbreðe. ne pið nan¹⁰ porlblich þing
penben me ne prenchen ut of þe¹¹ peie. þ ich am in begunnen to
ganne. ant unpurð¹² þ pite þu pel. me beoð þine porbeſ. for him
ane ich¹³ luuie. ant habbe to bileaue. þe pelt ant piſſeð þurh
hiſ¹⁴ pil. pinbeſ ant te peteres. ant al þ biſet iſ mit ſee ant¹⁵
mit ſunne. buuen ba ant bineoðen. al biſheð him¹⁶ ant beieð.
Teken þiſ þ he iſ ſo mihti ant ſo meinful.¹⁷ he iſ leoflukeſt
liſ ſor to lokin uppon. ant ſpoteſt to¹⁸ ſmeallen. ne hiſ ſpote
ſauur. ne hiſ almihti mihte.¹⁹ ne hiſ makeleſe luſſum lec ne

mei neauer licclin ⁱ⁰ ne aliggen. for he ne alið neauer. ah hueð
a in are. ant al þ in him lið. leafteð a mare. let quoð olibriuf
²¹ ne beoð þeof porb noht purð. ah an hpet pite þu ¹ bute ʒef
þu fpike ham. mi fpeorb fchal uorfpelten ² ant forfpolhen þi
flefch. ant þrefter beon forbernb on ³ berninbe glebeu. ah ʒef
þu pult leuen me þu fchalt ⁴ beon ini leouemon ant mi pif
ipebbet. ant pelben af lefbi al þ ich ipalb ah ant am of lauerb.
ich yeue þe pel ⁶ quoð heo of þine behefte. ah haue þu hit ant
ti luue. ⁷ for ich habbe a leouere þe ich nule for nan ꞉ leauen ⁸
ne leofen. þu fpencheft te to fpiðe. ant parpeft me ⁹ if pa fore
apei þine hpile. for al me if an þin olhnung ¹⁰ ant tin eie.
ichulle biteachen mi bobi to euereuch bitterneffe þ tu conft
biþenchen. ne beo hit neauer fo berf. to ¹² breienne to brehen
pið þon þ ich mote meibene mebe habben in heouene. brihtin
beibe for uf þe beorepurðe lauerb. ant ne brebich na beð for to
brehen for him. ¹⁵ he haueð his merke on me ifeilet. pið hif in
feil. ¹⁶ ne mei unc nopðer lif ne beað tpeamin atpa. Ya ¹⁷ quoð
he if hit fpa ꞉ neomeð hire fpiðe quoð he to ¹⁸ þe cpelleref.
ftrupeð hire fteorcnaket. ant hongeð hire on heh. ant beateð
hire bare bobi pið bittre befmen ²⁰ þe aparibe piðerlahen leiben
fpa luðerliche on ²¹ hire leofliche lich ꞉ þ hit brec oueral. ant
liðerebe ²² o blobe. þe eble meiben ahef hire heorte heaueb
(fol. 41) uppparb to þe heouene. ant feng on þeof bone. ²

Lauerb in þe if al þ ich hopie. halb me nu mi ³ pit fpa. ant mi
pil to þe. þ hit ne forpurðe naut. for ⁴ pa þ me bo me. ne leaf
þu neauer mine ifan. þef ⁵ feonbef of helle habben ne halben
hare hoker of ⁶ me. af ha palben ʒef ha mahten aparpen me.
ah ⁷ fpa ne fchulen ha me. ne nan oðer þ ariht luueð ⁸ þe.
heouenliche lauerb þi nome beo ibleffet. lauerb ⁹ loke to me.
ant haue merci of me. fofte me mi far. ¹⁰ fpa ant falue me
mine punben þ hit ne fem nopðer ne futeli omi famblant þ
ich berf brehe.
¹² Þe cpelleref leiben fpa luðerliche on hire lich ꞉ ¹³ þ tet
blob barft ut. ant ftrac abun of hire bobi ¹⁴ af ftream beð of

pelle. Olibriuſ þe luðere reue buten ¹⁵ reopðe hpil me ȝerbebe
hire þuſ ȝeomerliche ƺ' ȝeibe. Stute nu ant ſtep þine unpittie
porbeſ. ant hercne meiben mi reab. ant pel þe þe ſchal ipurðen.
alle þe þer peren peopmen ba ant pummen of reopðe ƺ' menben
þiſ meiben. ant ſumme of ham ſeiben. marherete. marherete
meiben ſo muche ƺ'¹ purð ȝef þu pel palbeſt. pa iſ uſ ꝥ pe iſeoð
þi ²² ſofte leofliche lich to luken ſpa labliche. peila ¹ pummon
hpuch plite þu leoſeſt ant forleteſt for þin ² miſbeleaue. þe
reue iſ reopliche prað. ant pule ipiſ ³ forbon þe. ah luue nu ant
lef him. ant tu ſchalt pummon ⁴ meaſt punne ant peole pelben.
O quoð M. preccheſ ⁵ unpeoten buten pit. peila hpet pene ȝe.
ȝef mi lich ⁶ iſ to loken. mi ſaple ſchal reſten mit te rihtpiſe. ⁷
Sorhe ant lichomeſ ſar. iſ ſaplene heale. ah leue ȝe ⁸ ich reabe
op. oþe luuenbe gobb mihti ant meinful ant ⁹ euch gobeſ ful.
þe hereð þeo ꝥ him to cleopeð. ant ¹⁰ heouene ȝeteſ openeð.
for op nullich iheren ne ¹¹ beien nane of oper gobeſ ꝥ bumbe
beoð ant beaue. ¹² ant blinbe bute mihte. pið monneſ honb
imakebe ¹³ ah þu purcheſ quoð ha to olibrium þe luðere þine
feber purkeſ þe ſonbeſ of helle. me þu heðene ¹⁵ hunb þe hehe
healent iſ min help. ant ȝef he ¹⁶ haueð iȝettet te mi licome to
luken ƺ' he pule hatele ¹⁷ reue arubben mi ſaple ut of þine
honben ant heouen ha to heouene. þah þu hongi me her. ant
tu ¹⁹ griſliche gra þu luðere liun lað gobb. þi mihte ſchal ²⁰
unmuchelin ant melten to riht noht. ant tu ſchalt beon ²¹ euer
in car. ant in ſorhe hpen ich gomeni pið gobb ²² ant glebie
buten enbe. he of preððe for neh ut (*fol.* 42) of hiſ ipitte.
ant beb ſpiðe hetterliche hongin hire ² on heh up herre þen
ha er pes. ant pið ſpeorb ſcharpe ³ ant pið eapleſ of irne hire
leofliche lich ronbin ant ⁴ renbin. ant heo biſeh up on heh ant
bigon to ſeggen.

⁵ Þelle hunbeſ lauerb habbeð bitrumet me. ant ⁶ hare reab
ꝥ heanið me. haueð al biſet me. ah ⁷ þu hehe healent beo umbe
me to helpen. arube reopðful gobb mi ſaple of ſpeorbeſ egge
ant of hunbeſ honb ⁹ for nabbich bute hire ane. leoſe me lauerb

.

ut of [10] þe liunes muð. ant mi meoke milðfchipe of þe [11] an-
hurnbe hornef. Glebe me pið þi gleo gobb. ant hope [12] of heale.
þ mi bone mote. þurh þurlin þe peolcne. Senð me þi fonðe
i culures iliche. þe cume me [14] to helpe. þ ich mi merðhaþ
mote piten to þe unpeommet. ant lef me ȝet lauerð. ȝef þi pil
if ifeon þ apariebe piht þ peorrið aȝein me. ant cuð þi mahte
on [17] me almihti goþþ. þ ich him ouercumen mahe. fpa [18] þ alle
meibenes eauer mare þurh me ;' þe mare truftin [19] on þe. beo
þi nome iblefcet alre bleo brihteft. in alre [20] porlbene porl aa
on ecneffe. amen.
  [21] Ƿpil þ M. fpec þuf ;' me toleac hire : fpa þ te uuele reue
for þe ftronge rune of þ bloði ftream [1] ne nan oðer þ ter pef
ne mahte for muchele grure [2] lokin piðeparbef. ah hubben
hare heauet þe hearbefte iheortet unber hare mantles. for þe
forhful far þ heo on hire ifehen. [4] ȝet fpec ant feiðe olibriuf
þe luðere. hpet bihalt meiben þ tu ne buheft to me. ne nult
habben milce ne [6] merci of þe feoluen ;' ȝe ne feleftu þi flefch
al toloken ant tolimet þurh þ ich hatte. ah buh nu ant bei
to me er [8] þu beie oberf beð ant oðrori. for ȝef þu ne beft no ;'
þu [9] fchalt fpelten þurh fpeorð ant al beon limel toloken. ant
[10] þenne ichulle tellen hpen þu al to torren art in euch [11] anef
fihðe þe fit nu ant fið þe alle þine feonepen. [12] Me hatele
hunð quoð ha þa. þah al fpa bo ;' me [13] ne fchenbeft tu napt.
hpen mi faple bið biuoren goðef fihðe in heouene. lutel if me
hpet me [15] ðo me. ant bi mi boði in eorðe. ah þe fchulbe
fcheomien [16] þu fcheomelefe fchucke. ȝef þu fcheome cuðeft.
þ [17] þulli mot halbeft pið a ȝung meiben. ant fpilleft [18] al þi
hpile ant ne fpebeft napiht. for ȝef ich prahte þe pil of þ
flefch. þ tu ueareft al af þu pult. pið ;' [20] mi faple fchulbe finken
al fpa af þin fchal to forhen in helle. ant for þi ichulle pel þ
mi flefch forfare her. þte fofte iefu cruni mi faple in felðhen
of (fol. 48) heouene. ant efter ðomef ðei ðo ham ba togeberef.
[2] to peolen ant to punnen þurh punienbe. he parð fo [3] prað þ
for neh pob he palbe ipurðen. beð bluef [4] cofte caften hire in

cpalm huſ. ant me ſpa bube. ſone. ⁵ ant peſ aſ þah hit pere þe
ſeoueðe time of þe bei ⁶ þ me broh hire þuſ into barckeſt pan.
ant purſt in ⁷ to punien. ant heo hef up hire honb ant bleſebe
al hire bobi pið þe hehe robe taken. aſ me lebbe hire ⁹ inparb.
ha bigon to bibben þeoſ bone to ure lauerb. ¹⁰ Deorepurðe
brihtin þah þine bomeſ berne beon: ¹¹ alle ha beoð buhti.
alle heouenliche þing. ant ¹² eorðliche baðe: buheð þe ant
beieð. þu art hope ant help ¹³ to alle þ te herieð. þu art
foſter ant feber to helpleſe chilbren. þu art ipebbebeſ peole.
ant pibepene ¹⁵ parant. ant meibenes mebe. þu art punne of þe
¹⁶ porlb. ihū criſt kinebern. gobb ikennet of gobb: ¹⁷ aſ liht
if of leome. loke lauerb to me. mi liſ. mi ¹⁸ luue. mi leouemon.
milce me þi meiben. min ¹⁹ ahne fleſchliche feber. bube ant
braf me apei hiſ ²⁰ anlepi bohter, ant mine freonb aren me
lauerb ²¹ for þi luue famen ant feonbeſ. ah þe ich habbe hehe
healent ba for feber. ant for freonb. ne forlet tu ¹ me napt
luuenbe lauerb. bihalb me ant help me. ant ² leſ me þ ich mote
leggen ehnen uppon þe luðere ³ unpiht þ peorreð aȝein me.
ant let me bemen pið ⁴ him brihtin of bome. he heanið ant
hateð me. ant ich ⁵ hit neauer nuſte þ he of min hearm hefbe.
ah ſpuche iſ hiſ cunbe. ant ſpa iſ ful of atter hiſ ontfule heorte
þ he hateð euch gob. ant euch hali þing. ant halepunbe is
him lað. þu art brihtin bomeſ mon of cpike ant ⁹ of beabe.
bem bituhen unc tpa. ne preð þu for na ſahe þ ich ſegge. for
a þing ich biſeche eauer. ant oueral ¹¹ þ tu pite to me mi
meiðhab unmerret. mi ſaple from ¹² ſunne. mi pit ant. mi piſ-
bom from þe pitleſe piht. ¹³ iþe iſ min healent al þ ich pilni.
beo þu al ibleſcet. ¹⁴ orbfrume ant enbe. ant ord aa on ecneſſe.
amen.

¹⁵ Þire uoſter mober peſ an þe frourebe hire. ant ¹⁶ com to
þe cpalmhus. ant brohte hire to fobe breb ¹⁷ ant burnes brunch
þ ha bilebe. heo þa. ant monie ma. ¹⁸ biheolben þurh an eyþurl
aſ heo beb hire beoben. ant ¹⁹ com ut of an hurne hihentliche
toparb hire an unpiht of helle on ane brake liche ſo griſlich

ꝥ ham²¹ agraſ prð ꝥ ha ſehen. ꝥ unſelhðe gliſtinbe. aſ hit ouergulb pere. hiſ lochkeſ ant hiſ longe berb ;' blikebe (*fol.* 44) al ogolbe. ant hiſ griſliche teeð ſemben of ſpart iru. ant² hiſ tpa ehnen ſteappre þene ſteorren ant þene ȝimſtaneſ ant brab aſ baſcinſ. in hiſ ihurnb heauet on eiðer⁴ half on hiſ hehe hokebe neoſe preaſte ſmeorðrinbe⁵ ſmoke ut ſmecche forcu-ðeſt. ant of hiſ ſpetepile muð ;'⁶ ſperklebe fur ut. ant lahte ut his tunge ſpa long. ꝥ he⁷ ſpoug hire al abuten hiſ ſpire. ant ſembe aſ þa ha ſcharp⁸ ſweorb of hiſ muð lahte. ꝥ gliſt-nebe aſ gleam beð. ant⁹ leitebe al oleie. ant al parð ꝥ ſtube of ſtrong. ant ſtarc ſtench.¹⁰ ant of þiſ ſchucke ſchabepe ſchiminbe anb ſchan al. he¹¹ ſtrahte him ant ſturebe toparb tiſ meoke meiben. ant¹² ȝeonebe mib his pibe geneop uppon hire ungeinliche.¹³ ant bigon to crahien. ant to crenchennut ſpire. as¹⁴ he ꝥ hire palbe forſpolhen mib alle. ȝeſ ha agriſen¹⁵ peſ of ꝥ griſliche gra nes napt muche punber. hire bleo bigon to blakien. for þe grure þe grap hire.¹⁷ ant for þe farlac offruht. forȝet hire bone ꝥ heo ibeben¹⁸ hefbe ſpa ꝥ ha moſte iſeon þen unſehen unpiht. ne¹⁹ napt ne þohte þeron ꝥ hire nu pere ituðet hire²⁰ bone. ah ſmat ſmertliche abun hire cneon to þe²¹ eorðe. an heſ hire honben on heh toparb heouene. ant prð þeoſ bone to criſte þuſ cleopebe.

¹ Vnſeheliche gobb euch gobeſ ful. hpaſ preððe iſ² ſpa gromelich ꝥ helle pare. ant heouenes ant alle³ cpike þingeſ cpakieð þer aȝeineſ. aȝein þiſ eiſful⁴ piht ꝥ hit ne eile me na-piht. help me mi lauerb.⁵ þu prahteſt ant pelbeſt alle porlb-liche þing. þeo þe heieð ant herieð in heouene. ant alle þe þingeſ ꝥ⁷ earbið in eorðe. þe fiſcheſ ꝥ i þe floſeſ fleoteð prð finneſ.⁸ þe fuheleſ þe fleon biðe luſte. ant al ꝥ ipraht iſ. pur-cheð⁹ ꝥ ti pil iſ. ant halt tine heſteſ bute mon ane. þe ſunne reccheð hire rune euch buten reſte. þe mone ant¹¹ te ſteorren he palcnið biðe peolcne. ne ſtutteð ne ne¹² ſtubgeð. ah ſturieð aa mare ne nohpiber of þe peie ꝥ tu haueſt ipraht¹³ ham ;' ne prencheð heo neaure. þu ſteoreſt te ſea¹⁴ ſtream ꝥ hit fleben

ne mot fir þan þu markebeſt. ¹⁵ þe pinbes. þe peberes. þe pubes.
ant te pettres. buheð ¹⁶ þe ant beieð. feonbes habbeð farlac.
ant englef of þin ¹⁷ eie. þe purmes ant te pilbe beor. þ on þeos
pilbe palbes punieð. libbeð efter þe lahen þ tu ham haueſt ¹⁹
iloket. huienbe lauerb. ant tu loki to me. ant help me. ²⁰ þin
honbi perc. for al min hope if on þe. þu herehebeſt helle ant
ouercome af kempe þene acurſebe gaſt. þ feonbeð to forbo
me. ah her me (*fol.* 45) nu ant help me for nabbich imi
nopcin nanes ² eunes elne bute þin ane. pið þif uuel pite me.
for ³ ich truſti al uppon þe. ant ti pil i' purði hit beorepurðe
lauerb. þ ich þurh þi ſtrencðe mahe ſtonben pið him. ⁵ ant his
muchele ouergat þ ich mote afallen. lop he ⁶ funbeð ſpiðe me
to forſpolhen. ant peneð for to beoren ⁷ me in to his balefule
hole þer he puneð inne. ah ⁸ oþi bliffule nome ich bleſci me
nuðe. ant broh þa enbelong hire ant þpertouer þreſter þe bere-
purðe ¹⁰ taken ! of þe beore robe. þ he onreſte. ant te brake
reſbe to hire mit tet ilke. ant ſette his fariliche ¹² muð ant
unmeaðeliche muchel. on heh on hire heaueb. ant rahte ut
hif tunge to þe ple of hire helen. ant ſpenbe hire in. ant
forſpalh into his pibe pombe. ah criſt to purðmunt. ant him
to praðerheale. þe robe taken arubbe hire reabliche. þ ¹⁷ heo
pes mib ipepnet. ant parð his bone fone. ¹⁸ ſpa þ his bobi to-
barſt omibheppeſ. ant te eble meiben ¹⁹ allunge unmerret.
pioðuten euereueh peom ²⁰ penbe ut of his pombe. herienbe on
heh hire hehe ²¹ healent in heouene. Af heo biheolb lokinbe
²² uppon hire riht half. þa ſeh ha hper ſet an ¹ unſehen unpiht
muchele bel blaccre þen euer eni ² blamon ſo griſlich þ ne
mahte hit na mon lihtliche areachen ant his tpa honben to
his cnurnebe cneon heteueſte ibunben. ant heo þa ha ſeh þiſ !
feng ⁵ to þonckin þus gobb. ant to herien hire hehe healent.

⁶ Brihteſt bleo of alle þ euer iboren peren bloſme iblopen ⁷
ant iboren omeibeneſ bobi ihū gobb ant gobbeſ bern. ibleſcet ⁸
beo þu euer. icham gomeful ant gleb lauerb of þi goblec. keiſer ⁹
of kingeſ brihtin unbeblich þu halbeſt ant heueſt up treope

bileaue. þu art palle of paiſbom. ant euch punne ¹¹ pakeneð
ant paxeð of þe. þu art englene peole. ꝥ pelbeſt ¹² ant piteſt
ham prouten ponunge. me gomeneð ant glebeð al of gaſtelich
murðe. me mihti gobb makeles ¹⁴ if ꝥ eni punber ꒒ ȝene ſeo
ich min bileaue blopinbe. ant ¹⁵ ichabbe iſehen þen feonb þe
penbe to forbon me ꒒ feol ¹⁶ efne atpa. ant felbe hu hiſ fule ſtench
ſtrac ant ſtrahte aȝeinparb. ichabbe iſehen þene þurſ of helle.
helles ¹⁸ pulf her aparpen. ant te monflahe iſlein. þe ſtronge ¹⁹
þurſ aſtoruen. ichabbe iſehen hiſ ouergart. ant his egebe ²⁰
orhel ferliche afallet. ich habbe iſehen þe robe þe arubbe me
ſo reblich of hiſ reopliche rake. hu ha ꝥ ²² balefulle purm ant
ꝥ bittre beſt makebe to berſten (fol. 46) ich habbe iſehen
hali ant halepunbi eoli. as bit lihte to me ꒒ ² ant ich me ſeolf
ſmelle of þe ſpote ihū. ſpottre þen euer ³ ani þing ꝥ is on
eorðe. ich habbe iſehen bliſſe ant ich ⁴ bliſſi me þrof. ipeole
ant ipunne is mi ꝥ ipunie. ant nes ⁵ me neauer ſpa pa ꒒ as me
is nu pel. þe ich hit þoncki ⁶ þolemobe lauerb. ich habbe abun
þe brake ibuſt. ant his ⁷ kenſchipe akaſt. ant he ſpelteð. ꝥ me
penbe to ſorſpolhen. ant ich am kempe ant he is crauant ꝥ
me penbe to ⁹ ouercumen. ah þe iþoncki þrof ꒒ ꝥ art kingene
king ¹⁰ echeliche icrunet. forhfule ant ſarie. ant ſunfule to turn.
¹¹ ponbrinbe ant precches ant panleſe piſſent. caſtel of ſtrencðe
aȝein þe ſtronge unpiht meibenes murhðe. ant ¹³ martirs crune.
mel ſeotel ſofteſt. ant gulbene ȝerbe alre golb ſmeateſt
gliſtinbe gimſtan of all ſeheliche þing. ant unſehelich baðe.
ſpoteſt ant ſpeteſt alre ¹⁶ ſchefte ſchuppent. þrumneſſe þreo
falb ꒒ ant anfalbte ¹⁷ hpeðere. þrile i þreo habes. ant i an
behſchipe. heh hali gobb euch gobeſ ful beo þu euer ant a
iheret ant iheiet. ¹⁹ bute linunge. AMEN. As ha hefbe
longe ²⁰ þus iheret ure lauerb com ꝥ griſliche gra. creopinbe
hire toparb. ant heolb hire bi þe fet. ant aſ an ſeorfule þing
ſariliche ſeibe. Margarete meiben ¹ inoh pa þu haueſt ibon me.
ne pine þu me na mare² pið þin eabi beoben. ꝥ tu bibbeſt ſo
ofte. for ha binbeð³ me ſpa ſare mib alle. ant makieð me ſo

unstrong. þ⁴ich ne fele mid me nanes cunnes strencðe. þu
haueſt grimliche ibroht mi broðer to grunde þen fleheſt
beouel of helle. þ ich on brake liche ſende. þe to ⁷ forſpolhen.
ant merrin prð hiſ muchele mihte þe mein of þi meiðhad. ant
makien þ tu nere na mare imong moncun imuneget on eorðe.
þu acpalbeſt him ¹⁰ mit te hali robe. ant me þu makeſt to
aſteoruen prð ¹¹ þe ſtrencðe of þine beoden þe beoð. þe ſo
imunde. ah ¹² leaf me gan leſði leaſteles ich þe bidde. þis milde
¹³ meiden margarete. igrap him þ ne agras hire napiht ant
hetefeſte toc him bi þe ateliche top. ant hef him up ant buſte
him abunriht to þer eorðe. ant ¹⁶ ſette hire fot uppon his
ruhe necke ant feng on þus ¹⁷ to ſpeokene. Stute nu earme
ſteorue ant ſpic ¹⁸ nuðe lanhure ſpikele ſparte beouel. þ tu ne
berue me na mare. for mi meiðhad ne helpeð þe ²⁰ napiht. for
ich habbe to helpe min hehe healent ²¹ in heouene. ant te
porlbeſ pelbent is ihper mi parant. Þa þu ſtrong pere. he pes
muchele (fol. 47) ſtrengre me to pitene. prð þis .' þa þubbe
ha uppon ² þe þurs feſte prð hire fot. prð euch an of þeos
porbeſ. ſtute nu uuele gaſt to gremien me mare. ſtute nu ⁴ þu
albe monſlahe. þ tu ne flea heonne forð criſtes ⁵ icorne. ſtute
nu platefule pibt to aſtenchen me. ⁶ prð þe ſtench þ of þi muð
ſtiheð. icham mi lauerbeſ ⁷ lomb. ant he is min hirbe. ant
icham his þral ant his ⁸ þeope to bon al þ his beore pil is. beo
he a ibleſcet ⁹ þe bliðe haueð imaket me in endeleſe bliſſe.
amen.

¹⁰ Þpil þ ha ſpec þus o þ ſpatepile piht. ſpa þer lihtinde com
in to þe cpalmhus a leome from ¹² heouene. ant ſembe aſ þah
ha ſehe iþe gliſtinde glem :' ¹³ þe beore robe. areachen to þe
heouene ant ſet a culure ¹⁴ þer on :' ant þus to hire cleopede.
Meiden eadi an art ¹⁵ tu margarete. for paraiſes ʒeten aren
ʒarepe iopenet þe nu. ant heo leat lahe to hire. leoue
lauerb. ¹⁷ ant þonckede him ʒeorne. prð inparde heorte þeos
meiden ant þ liht alei lutlen ant lutlen ant heo biturnde hire
þa ant epeð to þen unpiht. Cuð me quoð ha ²⁰ ſprðe. forcuðeſt

alre þinge cunðe þu beo. Lefði qð²¹ he leopſe þı fot of mı
necke. ant ſpa lanhure leoðe me²² meıben an eabıeſt þ̄ ıch eðı
mahe :/ ant ıch mot nebe. ant¹ neoðeles mın unpıl hıt ıs :/ to
bon al þ̄ tı pıl ıs. þe meıben² buðe ſpa leopſebe ant leoðebe a
lutel hıre hele ant he bıgon þuſ³ ſpetepetlıche to ſpeokene.
Þultu pıten luſſum lefðı⁴ hu ıch hatte. ah hpet ſo of mı nome
beo :/ ıch habbe efter⁵ bellzebub meſt monneſ bone ıbeon. ant
forſpolhen hare⁶ ſpınc. ant to aſpınðen ımaket. þe meðen þ̄ ha
moıı ȝer⁷ hefðen ımaket :/ þıs pıð ſume of mıne pıheleſ. ıch⁸
prenchte ham abun hpen ha left penðen ne neauer ȝet⁹ ne
mahte me na mon ouercomen bute þu nuðen þ̄ halbeſt¹⁰ me
ın bonðes ant haueſt ıblenð me her. ant art mı broðereſ¹¹ bone
ruffınes of helle. þe reheſt. ant te reaðpıſeſt of alle þeo ın helle.
Crıſt puneð ın þe. for þı þu purcheſt¹³ mıð us :/ al þ̄ tı pıl ıs.
ne napıht nartu pummon ılıch me¹⁴ þuncheð þ̄ tu ſchıneſt
ſchenre þen þe ſunne. ant ouer al þıne lımen þ̄ leıteð of leome.
þe fıngref ſpa freolıch me¹⁶ þuncheð ant ſo feıre ant ſo brıht
blıkınðe. þ̄ tu þe mıðe¹⁷ bleſceſt ant makeſt þe marcke of þe
beore robe. þ̄ reſðe¹⁸ me mı broðer :/ ant me pıð bale bonðes :/
bıtterlıche¹⁹ bınðeſt. þ̄ ıch lokı ne meı. ſpa þ̄ lıht leomeð ant
leıteð²⁰ me þuncheð. þu fıkeſt quoð ha ful þıng ah cuð me²¹ þ̄
ıch eſkı. pumme lefðı qð he þa :/ pa ıs me mıne lıues. ²² bute
ıch peorrı a pıð þe rıhtpıſe. of þe unſelıe ſun (ſol. 48) fule me
þuncheð ıch am al ſıker. ah þe goðe ıch am bıfılıche abuten.
ant heom ı folhı neoðelukeſt. þ̄ cunnıð to³ beon cleane pıðuten monneſ man ant fleoð fleſches fulðen. ȝef ıch mahte eypeıſ
makıen ham to fallen ant⁵ fulen ham ſeoluen. Monıe ıch
habbe ıparpen þ̄ penðen⁶ mıne pıheleſ pıterlıche et ſterten.
ant on þıſſe pıſe. ⁷ ıch leote oðer lıpıles a cleane mon :/ punıen
neh a cleane pummon. þ̄ ıch toparð ham ne parpe ne ne peorrı.
⁹ ah leote ham ıpurðen. ıch leote ham talkın ant tauelın¹⁰ of
goðlec ant treoplıche luuıen ham. pıðuten uuel pılnung¹¹ ant
alle unpreſte pılles. þ̄ erðer of oðeres as of hıs¹² ahne beo truſtı.
ant treoplıche to pıtene. ant te ſıkerure¹³ beon to ſıtten

togeberes ant gomenin bi hain ane. þenne ¹⁴ þurh þis fikerlec
feþhe ich earſt uppon ham ant ſcheote ¹⁵ ſpiðe bernlich ant
punbi er ha piten hit. p̅ið ſpiðe attri halepi. hare unparie
heorte. lihtliche on alre earſt. p̅ið ¹⁷ luueliche lates. p̅ið ſteape
bihalbunge eiðer on oðer. ¹⁸ ant p̅ið plohe ſpeche ſputte to
mare. ſpa longe þ ha ¹⁹ tollið togeberes ant toggið. ant þenne
þubbe ich in ham ²⁰ luueliche þohtef on earſt hare unþonckes
ant ſpa paxeð ²¹ þ pa þurh þ ham hit þuncheð gob. ant þenne
ant hpen ha ²² leteð me. ant he letten me napt. ne ne ſtorið
hamſeolf ⸱⸴ ¹ ne ne ſtonbeð ſtrongliche aȝein ⸴⸴ ich leabe ham iþe
leinen. ant ² iþe labliche lake of þe ſuti funne. ȝef ha et ſtonben
³ pulleð mine unpreſte prenchef ant mine ſpikele ſpengef ⸴⸴
preſtlin ha moten ant piðerin p̅ið ham ſeoluen. ah me a-
keaſten ha ue mahen. er ha ham ⁶ ſeolf ouercumen. Lað is
me ant neoðelef neblunge i bo ⁷ hit cuðe þe hu ha mahen beſt
ouercumen me. leopſe me ant ⁸ leoðe me lefði þe hpile. ant ich
þe pile ſegen.

⁹ þif beoð þe pepnen þ me purſt punbeð ant. piteð ¹⁰ ham
unpeommet ant ſtrengeð ham ſtaleparblukeſt aȝein me. ant
aȝein ham ant hare pake luſtes. ¹² þ beoð eoten meokeliche
ant bruncken meokeluker. ¹³ bon þ fleſch iſum berf. ant neauer
ibel. monne bone p̅ið hare ahne. ant beobefule þohtef þ ha
ſchulen þenchen. ¹⁵ bimong hare benen ant aȝein uupreſte
þohtef þenchen hit is þurh me ⸴⸴ þ hare luſt leabeð ham to
purchen to punbre. þencheu ȝif ha beieð to me ⸴⸴ to hu ¹⁸ bittre
beſt ha beieð ant hpas luue ha leofeð þ luffum ¹⁹ þing ⸴⸴ meiðhab meibeneſ menſke. ant te luue ⸴⸴ of þen ²⁰ luueliche lauerb
of heouene ant te luffum cpen englene lefði ant heanlungeſ
makeð ham p̅ið heouènlich hirð ant unmenſkeð hamſeolf
bimong eorðlich (fol. 49) men ant forleoſeð þe luue. napt
ane on heh in heouene ah ² of lah ec in eorðe. ant makieð þe
englef to murnin ant uſ ³ muche murhðe to laben ſo lube. þe
feoð ham lihten ſpa ⁴ lah of ſo ſpiðe heh. from þe heſte in
heouene to þe laheſte in helle. þis ha moten ofte munnen bi

ham feoluen. ⁶ þenchen hu fparc [þing ant hu futi if funne.
þenchen ⁷ of helle pa. of heouenrichef punne. ant hare ahne ⁸
beð ant brihtines munegin ilome. ant te grifle ant te grure ⁹
þe brð et te bome þenchen þ te flefchef luft alrð fprðe fone. þe
pine þeruore leafteð a mare. ant tenne ¹¹ fome agulteð eapiht.
gan anan forðriht þ ha ne ¹² firften hit napiht to fchapen hit
ifchrifte. ne beo ¹³ hit no fo lutel. ne fo liht funne þ if under
funne þinge me laðeft þ me eorne ofte to fchrift of hif funnen. for lutle ich mei makien to muchelin unmeaðeliche ȝef
me hut ant heleð hit. ah fone fo hit ifhapet ¹⁹ is birepfinde
ifchrifte. þenne fcheomeð me. ant þerprð ¹⁸ fleo ham from
fchudrinde as ich ifchend pere. þah ¹⁹ fo forð ant fo feor ha
mahen ftepen eft in fofteliche ²⁰ to luuien. þ ha nanef peis ne
fchulen ftepen hare ²¹ heorte ne et ftunten ne et ftonden þe
ftrencðe ²² of mine fpenges. hpil ha fomet beoð :' nis þer bote
' nan :' bute fleon þenne. þ nopðer neophper ane mib ² oðer ne
feon ham ne fompnin ne fitten to geberes. ³ prð uten pitneffe.
þe mahe ifeon hpet ha don ant ⁴ heren hpet ha feggen. ȝef
ha þuf ne letteð me napt ⁵ ah þauieð ant þolieð ant peneð þah
to et prenchen ich ⁶ leabe ham prð leaf luue lutlen ant lutlen
into fo ⁷ beoþ bung þ ha bruncneð þerin. ant fprechi in ham
fprekef of luftef fpa luðere. þ ha forberneð in prð ant þurh ⁹
þe brime ablindeð. þ ha nabbeð fihðe nan :' ham feoluen to
bifeonne. þe mein of ham melteð þurh þe ¹¹ heate ant forpurðeð
hare pit ant peorreð hare pifdom ¹² fpa þ nulleð ha napt piten.
þ tat ha ahten to piten ¹³ pel. loke nu hpunder. ha beoð fo
cleane ouercumen ¹⁴ ant fpa ich habbe ablend ham þ ha blindlunge gað ¹⁵ ant forfeoð gobb ant ham feoluen forȝeoteð. fpa
þ ha luðerliche hpen ha leaft peneð ferliche falleð. fule ant
fenniliche i flefchliche fulðen. for a luft þ alrð man hondhpile
leofeð ba þe luue of gobb ant te þorlbef purðfchipe ¹⁹ ah þeo
þ ftalepurðe beoð ant ftarke to ȝein me. fpa þ heo ham ²⁰ prð
me ant mine prenchef. pecchinde ham perien. fo ²¹ uuel me
þuncheð þrof. þ al ich am breori aðet ha beon ²² þurh me

iboruen. ant am in hare bebbef fo bifi ham a (*fol.* 50) buten
þ fummes peis ha fchulen ham flepinde fulen ah þe robe mercke
merreð me oueral. ant mefc³ et ten ende. ant mit tis ilke
bigon to ʒeien ant to ʒuren. ⁴ Margarete meiden to hpon fchal
ich ipurðen. mine pepnen aren allunge aparpen. ʒet pere hit⁶
þurh a mon as is nu þer a pummon. þis ʒet þuncheð me⁷ purft.
þ al þ cun þ tu art of icumen beoð in ure bondes. ant tu art
et broken ham alre pundre meaft þ tu þe ane⁹ haueft ouer-
gan þi feber ant ti mober. meies ba ant mehen. ¹⁰ ant al þe ende
þ tu ant heo habbeð in ierbet ant crift ane haueft ¹¹ icoren
to leouemon ant to lauerd. Beateft us ant bindeft ¹² ant
to beaðe forbemeft. pei pake beo pe nu ant noht purð¹³
mid alle hpen a meiden ure muchele ouergart þuf afalleð. ¹⁴
Step quoð heo fari piht ant fei me hper þu¹⁵ meft puneft.
of hpet cun þu art icunien. ant ti cunde¹⁶ cuð me ant þurh
hpaf hefte heani ʒe ant harmeð hare perkef¹⁷ ah fei me feli
meiden hponne is te ileanet. i þine leoðebeie limen fo ftalepurðe ftrencðe. of hpet cunde cumeð þe þi luue ant tin
bileaue. þ lerð me fo lahe. Cuð²⁰ me ant ken me hpi þe
porldes peldent puneð in þe²¹ ant hu he com pummon to
þe. ant ichulle makien þe par of alle mine piheles. Step þe
fteorue ant¹ ftille beo þin efcunge. ʒe nart tu napt purðe
to heren² mi ftefne apariebe ful piht. ant hure⁚to under-
ftonden³ fo berne þing ant fo derf: of godes bihelneffe ant
hpet⁴ fo ich am þurh godef grace ich hit bo ant am pilʒeoue
unofferuet. þ he me haueð iʒetted. for to ʒelden hit⁶ him
feoluen ah fpiðe cuð me ant ken : þ ich efki efter. ⁷
Sathanaf þe unfeli þ for his prude : of paraif lihte ⁸ fo lahe
he is keifer ant king icrunet of us alle.⁹ ant hperto fchuld
i tellen þe ant mi tale tealin luffum lefdi of ure cunde ant
ure cun. þ tu coft te feolf ifeon. in iamef¹¹ ant imembref
bokef ibreuet. fpuch farlac ich fele ant for¹² fihðen þ ich
ifeo. crift fechen to þe. þ fpeoken i ne bar¹³ napt. ah biueri
ant darie drupeft alre þinge. þah hpen¹⁴ þu piten pult. pe

ÞE MEIDEN ANT MARTYR.

luueð bi þe lufte. alre mesten bel. [15] ebie meiden ant ure peief
beoð abunen pið þe pinbes. [16] ant beoð a pakere to purchen al
þ pa. þ pe eauer mahen moncun ant meaft rihtpife men ant
meibenes af þu art. for ihū crift gobef bern pef of meiden [19]
iboren ant þurh þe mihte of merðhab: pes moncun iboren.
[20] binumen ant birefben us al þ pe ahten nu þu paft [21] lefbi þ þu
pite palbeft. hper pe meft punieð. ant hpi pe meft [22] heaneð ant
hatieð þe meibenes. ȝet ȝef þu pite pult hpi pe peorrð meaft
rihtpife þeinef ich onfperie. for (fol. 51) onbe þ et euer ant aa
ure heorte. pe piten. ha beon iprahte [2] to ftihen to þe ftube. þ
pe of feollen. ant us hokerliche [3] þuncheð ant fpiðe hofles þrof.
fpa þe teone ontent us. þ [4] pe ipurðeð poðe þurh þe grome þ
us gromeð aa pið þe [5] gobe. þ is ure cunbe. þ ich þe fchulbe
tellen. ant beon [6] forhful ant fari of euch monnef felhðe. ant
gomenin: [7] hpen he gulteð. ant neauer mare ne beo gleabe
bute for uuel ane [8] þis is ure cunbe makelefe meiben. ah beore
brihtines lomb: [9] leoðe me a lutel ant leopfe lefbi þi fot þ fit
me fo fare [10] ich halfi þe ogobef nome heh heouenlich feber
ant on ihc̄ [11] half his an fulliche fune. mon ne pummon ne
mahe ne [12] auer mare parpen me heonne ant tu brihte burbe
binb [13] me in eorðe. ant ne parp þu me napt neoðer into helle.
[14] for falomon þe pife. hpil he her punebe. bitunbe us [15] in ane
tunne. ant comen babilones men. ant penben [16] for to habben
golb horb ifunben ant breken þ feat. ant pe [17] forð ant fulben
þa: þe pibneffe of þe porlb.   Stille beo þu [18] ftile earmeft alre
fteorue. ne fchaltu albe fchuke motin pið me na mare. ah flih
forhfule þing ut of min [20] ebfihðe ant bef þiber as þu mon ne
berue na mare. pið [21] þ ilke þe eorðe to tpembe ant bitunbe
him ant he rarinbe [22] rab ruglinge into helle.   Ine marhen
fenbe olibriuf [1] þe luðere his men to bringen hire biuoren him.
ant heo blefcebe hire ant com balbeliche forð. ftriken men
þiberparb þea: [3] of eauer euch ftrete for to feo þe feorhe þ
me palbe [4] leggen uppon hire leofliche bobi. ȝef ha to þe reuef
[5] reab ne buhe ne beie.   Meiben qð he. margarete ȝet ibibbe

D

ant bodie þ tu purche mi pil ant purge⁷ mi mapmez. ant te
tibe ant te time þ tu iboren pere ?⁸ fchal beon iblefcet. Nai
qð ha ne kepich napt þat⁹ me blefci fpa. ah hit pere þi gein
þ tu þe geft unblefcet. ant ti gob baðe efter blefcunge ga. ant
heie¹¹ gobb almihti heh heouenlich feber. ant his feolcuðe¹²
fune. þe is foð mon. ant gobb noðelatere. ah þu purgeft¹³
pitlefe pihtes as þu art purðe. blobles ant banles¹⁴ bumbe ant
beaue. ant ȝet tu purcheft purfe. for þe unfehene unpihtes
punieð ham pröinnen ant tu as¹⁶ þine lauerbes. luueft ham. ant
heieft. Þim bigon¹⁷ to gremien ant o grome grebbe. ftrup-
peð hire fteorc¹⁸ naket. ant heoueð hire on heh up þ ha
hongi to mebe.¹⁹ for hire hokeref. ant ontenbeð hire bobi mib
bearninbe taperes. þe brieueles unbuhti fpa buben fone²¹ þ te
hube fnap hpit fpartete as hit fnarchte. ant²² barft on to
bleinen þ hit araf up ? oueral. ant hire (fol. 52) leofliche lich
refchte of þe leie. fpa þ alle remben² þ on hire fofte fiben ?
ifehen þet reopðe. ant heo bigon bauies bone. Heh heouenlich gobb pið þe halpunbe fur of þe hali gaft moncunne froure.
fure min heorte ant let te lei of þi luue leiten mine lenben.
ȝet him cpeð⁶ olibriuf reuene luðereft. lef meiben ini reab.
purch þ⁷ ich pilni ear þen þu þi lif? luðerliche forlete. Luðerliche ich huebe quoð margarete ȝef ich þe ilefbe.⁹ ah ȝef i
þuf beie mi faple is beorepurðe ant beore in¹⁰ to eche liue. þu
fpencheft te fpiðe ant ne fpebeft¹¹ napiht. ne mahtu ne þin
unpiht napiht purchen¹² on me meiben an as ich am. ah per-
gið op feoluen.¹³ an lauerb haueð mine luuen funberlich ifeilet.
ant haueð to mi ȝimftan þ ich ȝettebe him? iȝarket ant¹⁵ iȝeuc
me kempene crune. þa parð þe reue pob¹⁶ ant beb o pobe pife
ant o great praðde bringen forð¹⁷ a uet. ant fullen hit of pettre.
ant binben hire baðen þe¹⁸ fet. ant te honben. anb buften
hire into þe grunbe. þat¹⁹ ha beð brehbe ant bruncnebe þerinne. me bube fone²⁰ as he bon het. ant heo biheolb on heh
up. ant cleopebe toparb heouene. Alre kingene king brec nu²¹
mine bonbes. þ ich ant alle. þ hit ifeoð. heien¹ þe ant herien.

þis peter mote purðen me punfum. ant² fofte. ant lef me þ
hit to me ;˙ beð beo of bliffe. ant³ fulht of fonftan. healunge
ant leome of echelich heale. ⁴ cume þe hali gaft o culures lich
þ oþi bliffule nome blefci þeof pettres. feftne við fulht. mi
faple to ⁶ þe feoluen. ant mit teof ilke pettres peofch me við-
innen. ant parp from me apei euuer euch funne. ant bring ⁸ me
to þi brihte bur ;˙ brudgume of punne. Ich unðeruo ⁹ her
fulht o beore brihtnes nome. ant on hif beorepurðe funef ant
o þes hali gaftes. ¹⁰ an gobb in goblec itunet. ant untobealet.
Nefðe ha bute ¹¹ ifeid fpa ;˙ þ al þe eorðe ne bigon to cpakien.
ant com ¹² a culure beorninde briht af þah ha berude. ant
brohte ¹³ a guldene crune ant fette oþ feli meidenes heauet.
við ¹⁴ þ ilke burften ant breken hire bondes. ant heo as ¹⁵
fchene as fchininde funne peude up þrof finginde aloft ¹⁶ fong.
þ dauið þe pitege prahte feor þer biuoren. crift ¹⁷ to purðmunt. Mi luffum lauerd qð ha he cubeð as king ¹⁸ þ he rixleð
arıht. feirlec ant ftrencðe beoð his fchrudes ¹⁹ ant igurd he is
ham on þ ha cumeliche faren ant femliche fitten. Cum qð
þe culure við fchillinde ftefne ant ²¹ ftih to þe peolen ant to þe
punnen in heouene. eadi pere þu ²² meiden þa þu chure meiðhad þe is cpen of alle mih(*fol.* 53)tes for þi þu fchalt aa buten
ende bruken bliffe. amen.

² Oþ ilke time turnden to ure lauerd fif þufent men. ³ ȝet
viðuten itald children ant pummen þ alle peren anan ⁴ riht o
criftes kinepurðe nome. as þe reue het ;˙ hefðes ⁵ bicoruen in an
burh of armenie caplimet inempnet. ⁶ alle herıende godd við
up aheuen ftefne. ant ftihen alle ⁷ martirs við murhðen to
heouene. Þe reue rudnede ⁸ al o grome fpa him gromede. ant
parð fpa prað. ant fpa apeð. þ he o ⁹ poðe pife bemde hire te
deaðe ant het on hat heorte. þ ¹⁰ me hire heauet við fchim-
mende ant fcharp fpeord to tpemde from þe bodie. leiden
honden on hire. þeo þ ihaten ¹¹ peren ant bunden hire þ tet
blod barft ut et te neiles. ant ¹³ viðuten þe burh lebden to
bihefden. Meiden quoð ¹⁴ malcus ftreche uorð þi fpire fcharp

speorð to unberfonne for ich mot ti bone beon. ant þ̄ me is pā
fore ¹⁶ ȝef ich mahte þer prð. for ich ifeo gobb feolf mið his ¹⁷
eaði engles bitrumen þe abuten. abið me broðer ¹⁸ þenne qð
ha hpil þ̄ ich ibibbe me. ant biteache mi gaft ¹⁹ ant mi bobi
baðen to ro ant to refte. Ich bibbe qð he þ̄ tu ²⁰ bo balbeliche hpil þe gob likeð. ant heo bigon on hire cneon to cneolin
abun ant bliðe prð þeos bone ²¹ ber on heh iheuen up honben
toparð heouene. ¹ Drihtin leobes lauerð þah þine runes
berne ² beon ant berne alle ha beoð buhti. me is beað ³ ibemet
her nu. ant prð þe lif ileanet. þi milbe milce ⁴ ich þoncki hit.
þu folckes feber of frumfchaft fchupteft al þ̄ ifchapen is. þu
pifeft pruhte of alle. markebeft eorðe. þu ftoref mon of fea
ftream. þu piffent ⁷ ant pelbent of alle pihtes þ̄ iprahte beoð
fehliche. ant ⁸ unfehliche. buh þine earen healinbe gobb ant
bei to mine benen ich bibbe ant bifeche þe. þ̄ art me peole ¹⁰
ant punne. þ̄ hpa fo eauer boc prit of mi liflabe. oðer ¹¹ biȝet
hit ipriten. oðer halt hit ant haueð ofteft ¹² an honbe. oðer
hpa fo hit eauer rebeð. oðer þene rebere bliðeliche luftnið.
pelbent of heouene purðe ham ¹⁴ alle fone hare funnen for-
ȝeuene. Hpa fo oni nome makeð chapele. oðer chirche. oðer
ifinbeð in ¹⁶ ham liht. oðer lampe. þe leome ȝef ham lauerð
ant ¹⁷ ȝette him of heouene. iþe huf þer pummon pineð ochilbe
fone fo heo munnið mi nome hihentliche help ¹⁹ hire ant iher
hire bene. þ̄ iþe hus þ̄ ne beo iboren nan ²⁰ mifbilimet bern.
noþðer halt ne houeret. noðer ²¹ bumbe ne beaf. ne iberuet
of beoulen. ah hpa fo eauer ²² mi nome munegið. ant hit haueð
hit ofte imuðe (*fol.* 54) luueliche lauerð et te lafte bome
ales ham from beaðe.
² Pið þis þa þuhte hit as þah a þunre bunebe ant com ³ a
culure briht as þah ha bernbe from heouene. ⁴ pið a robe
leitinbe of liht ant of leome. ant te meiben buuelunge feol
bun to þe eorðe ant com þe culure ant aran hire ant rihte
hire up ⸱⸱ pið þe robe. ant feibe hire fpeteliche to ⸱⸱ ⁷ pið fpoteft
alre ftefne. Eaði art tu meiben bimong ⁸ alle pummen. þe

ÞE MEIDEN ANT MARTYR.

eoli halpunðe ant halfum þ tu haueft ifoht [9] efter :' ant alle
funfule men imuneget i þin eaði beoben [10] ant iþine benen. Bi
me feolf ich fperie. ant bi min heouenlich hirð. þ tine beoben
beoð þe treopliche ituðet. [11] ant for alle þeo iherb. þ tu fore
ibeben haueft. ant muche [13] mare is ȝeuen to þeo :' þ tin nome
munnið. ant iȝettet [14] ham moni þing þ nis napt nu imuneget.
ant hper [15] fo þi boði :' oðer eni of þine ban beoð. oðer boc of
þi pine. cume þe funfule mon ant legge his muð þer up [17] on
ich falue him his funnen. ant ne fchal nan unpiht [18] punien
iþe panes þer þi martirðom is ipriten inne. ah alle of þe hus
fchulen gleðien igoðes grið. [20] ant igafteliche luue. ant alle þ
te biððeð to ȝarckin ich ȝetti [21] ham of hare bruchen bote.
ant tu art eaði ant te ftuðe þ [22] tu on refteft. ant alle þeo þ
þurh þe :' fchulen turnen to me. [1] cum nu forð burðe to þi
bruðgume. cum nu leof to þi lif. [2] for ich copni þi cume.
brihteft bur abit te. leof hihe [3] to me cum nu to mi kineðom.
leaf þe leoðe fpa lah. ant [4] tu fchalt pelðen pið me al þ ich ah.
alre burðe brihteft. [5] þe ftefne ftutte. ant heo ftoð up. ant
bigon to bibðen. þeo þ [6] hire abuten peren. ant hire beað bi-
peopen. þ ha fchulðe [7] þolien. ant feiðe leteð ant leaueð oper
nurð. ant oper labliche [8] bere. ant gleðieð alle pið me þ me
goð unnen for ȝe habbeð [9] iherð ȝef ȝe hercneben ariht hpet
te behe healent [10] haueð me bihaten. ant af ȝe luueð opfeolf.
luueliche ich [11] leare op. þ ȝe habben mi nome muchel ine
munðe. for [12] ichulle biððen for þeo bliðeliche in heouene. þe
ofte [13] munneð mi nome ant munegeð in eorðe. pið bliðe
heorte [14] bereð me genge. for to herien þe king. þe haueð
icoren [15] me þorlbef pruðte anð pelðent al is :' þe ich þoncki
þrof. [16] þe ich heie ant herie heouenlich healent. for þi beorepurðe nome ich habbe iðrohen nopcin. ant nume beað nuðen.
ant tu nim me to þe goðð. of al þ goð is ortfrume ant [19] enðe.
beo þu a iblefcet. ant ti bliffule fune iefu crift. bi [20] his nome
pið þe hali gaft. þ glit of inc baðen. þreoualð. ant tað an
untoðealet in an haðes. totpemet [22] in hehfchipe. untoðealet

ʒeiet. ant itunet an gobb in (*fol.* 55) magin. purðfchipe ant
purðmunt² purðe to þe ane from porlbe into porlbe³ aa on
ecneffe. Efter þeos bone þa beh ha þe fpire.⁴ ant cpeð to þe
cpellere. bo nu broðer hihentliche þ̄ te is⁵ ihaten. Nai quoð
he nulle ich no. for ichabbe iherb hu brihtines beore muð
haueð pið þe imotet. Þu moft quoð⁷ þ̄ meiben neblunge bon
hit. for ʒef þu ne beft no :′ ne⁸ fchaltu habben pið me bale of
heouene riche. Ant⁹ he pið þ̄ ilke hef up. hateleft alre pepne.
ant fmat fmertliche abun. þ̄ te bunt befde in. ant tet fcharpe
fpeorb. ant¹¹ eke fmart. fcher hire bi þe fchulbren. ant
fahebe hire¹² þurhut. ant te bobi beibe. ant beh to þer eorðe.
þe gaft¹³ anan riht fteh up. in to þe ftirrebe bur bliðe to
heouene. Þe þ̄ te bunt ʒef ʒeibe. lube ftefne. brihtin bo me
merci¹⁵ of þis bebe. of þis funne lauerb loke me nu falue ant
feol¹⁶ abun for farlac on hire riht halue. Comen lihtinbe þa þe
engles of heouene. ant feten. ant fungen on hire¹⁸ bobi bi-
lehpit. ant blefceben hit. þe feonbef þ̄ ter peren¹⁹ bebliche
iboruen fengen to ʒeien. Margarete meiben²⁰ leoðe nuðen
lanhure ant leopfe ure bonbes. pe beoð pel²¹ icnapen. þ̄ nis
nan lauerb. bute gobb. þ̄ tu on leueft.²² Turnben þa þurh
þis to crifte fpiðe monie. ant comen.¹ bumbe ant beaue to
hire bobi as hit lei.² ant botneben alle. þe englef as ha beren
þe³ faple in hare barmes fihen to heouene. ant fungen as⁴ ha
ftihen up pið fpoteft ftefne. fanctuf. fanctuf. fanctuf. et cet.
⁵þ̄ is. hali is. hali is. þe lauerb of heouene riche por⁶bes. heouene
if ful. ant eorðe of þine purðfule peolen.⁷ alre pihte pelbent.
in hehneffe. heal us. iblefcet beo þe⁸ bernes cume þe cum
obrihtines nome heale in hehneffe. pið þ̄ :′ þa bigunnen to
þeoten ant to ʒellen. ant tuhen¹⁰ alle to hire bobi. þe untrume
peren ant hefben hare¹¹ heale. Cum ich theochimuf ant toc
hire leofliche lich¹² ant ber hit into a burh of antioche. pið
murhðe unimete. ant bube hit igraue ftan. in hire granbame
hus þ̄¹⁴ pes icleopet clete. ich ab pel to piten þif for ipine¹⁵ of
prifun þer ha pes iput in. ich hire fluttunge fonb :′¹⁶ ant flefch-

þE MEIDEN ANT MARTYR.

liche sobe. ant ich iseh hwer ha faht. wið þe [17] feorliche feont. ant hire bone wes þ ich hit write on [18] bocfelle. ant hire liflabe al lette bon o leaue. ant sende hit [19] soðliche ipriten wiþe ʒont te worlbe.

[20] Þus þe eabie meiben margarete binome. iþe moneð þ on ure lebene is. alb englifch efterhð inempnet. [21] iuliuf olatin oþe twentuðe bei wið tintreo beibe. ant (*fol.* 56) penbe from weanen to eche punnen. to lif þ a lefteð buten [1] balefið. to bliffen buten wa: euer lestinbe.

[3] Alle þeo þe þis heortelıche habbeð iherb. in oþer [4] beoben þe bliðeluker munnıð þis meiben. þat [5] heo wið þe ilke bone þ heo beb on eorðe. bibbe ʒet for op [6] iþe bliffe of heouene. þer ha fchineð seoneualb [7] fchenre þen þe funne. ısı. ant ıselhðe. mare þen eni muð [8] hit cuðe munnen. i þ englene hirb fingeð aa unfulet. [9] þ mon ne pummon. ne mei þat is flefch [10] fulet. þ þe bituhen þe engles þurh hire ernbunge [11] moten ʒet iseon hire. ant iheren hire fingen. amen. [12] Gret wurðe gobb feber:/ ant hıf fune ısemet. þe hali [13] gaft iheiet. þeos þreo in an iþeinet of engles. ant [14] of eorðliche inen a buten enbe. amen.

SEINTE MARGARETE

ÞAT HOLI MAIDE.

MS. Harl. 2277. fol. 84. b.

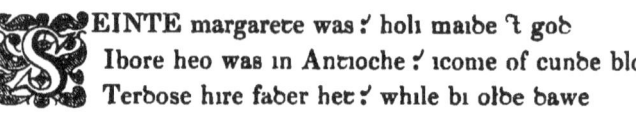EINTE margarete was ✢ holi maide ꝥ god
Ibore heo was in Antioche ✢ icome of cunde blod
Terdose hire fader het ✢ while bi olde dawe
Patriarch he was wel heȝ ✢ ꝥ maister of þe lawe
5 He ne bileouede on ihū crist noȝt ✢ for he heþene was
Margarete his ȝunge douȝter ✢ ipaid þerwiþ noȝt nas
For hire hurte dar anon ✢ cristene to beo
Þe false godes heo het deuelen ✢ þᵗ heo miȝte albai iseo
f. 85 Of seint steuene heo hurde telle ✢ ꝥ seit Laurenz also
10 Hou in strong martirdom ✢ hi were to deþe ido
ꝥ of oþer martirs ek ✢ þᵗ þolede pyne here
Þeo ne wilnede noȝt so moche ✢ as to beo here fere
¶ Þis maide was þo hire moder deide ✢ ȝung ꝥ tendre ynouȝ
Þire fader hit sone underȝat ✢ þᵗ heo to cristendom drouȝ
15 Þe makede for hire deol ynouȝ ✢ fram home he gan hire sende
To a norice to wardi hire wel ✢ hire hurte for to wende
Viftene myle fram Antioche ✢ þᵗ maide clene ꝥ hende
In þe londe of Asye ✢ isend was in þon ende
Þis ȝunge maide was clene ynouȝ ✢ þo heo fram home wende
20 Of viftene ȝer heo was uneþe ✢ þo hire fader hire þider sende
Hit was ek tuo hondred ȝer ✢ ꝥ four score ꝥ fyue
Eft þᵗ god was idore ✢ to bringe ous out of pyne
¶ Liþer was þemperor Diocletian ✢ .... (*an erasure*) ....

Liþer was his felawe ek :/ þt het maximian
25 Hi bestruyþe alle criftene men :/ ʒt wel wiþe soʒte
Anɔ when hi miʒte eni fynde :/ in stronge beþe hẽ broʒte
Juftises hi makeþe meni on :/ þt wenþe alonþe wiþe
Forto siche criftene men :/ ʒt quelle in eche siþe
þt on was ihote Olibrius :/ þt into Afie wenþe
30 to siche þerout criftene men :/ as þemperour hĩ senþe
¶ Þis ʒunge maiþe þt was þere :/ in on enþe of Afie
Priuerliche niʒt ʒt day :/ in our louerd gan crie
þt he senþe hire stedeuaft hurte :/ ʒt in our leueþi marie
Wiþoute feyntife in hire name :/ þe tourmentz of þeþe drie
35 þe norice þt hir habþe in warþe :/ louede hire ynouʒ
Ac heo nas noʒt ahwar :/ to whan hire hurte drouʒ
. Þis clene maiþe þt was so ʒung :/ of vyftene ʒer vneþe
Heo wilneþe euere to beo iþo :/ for oure louerdes [name] to þeþe
Hir norice hir senþe ofte abai :/ wiþ hire schip afelþe
40 to witie hire schip wiþ oþer maiþenes :/ þt were of hir elþe
¶ As þis maiþe wiþ hire schep :/ abai afelþe was
. Þis iuftise Olibrius :/ þerforþ com bi cas
Þe clene maiþe he behulþ :/ heo þoʒte hĩ clene ʒt fair ynouʒ
Anon riʒt in fole sone :/ his hurte to hir drouʒ
45 Him longeþe sore after hire :/ his men after hire he senþe
ʒt het hẽ hafteliche :/ þt hi after hire wenþe
If heo were of gentil blod :/ his wyf heo scholþe beo
ʒt wiþ gret nobley leþe hire lyf :/ ʒt if heo nere noʒt freo
Bugge he wolþe hire þeore yiiouʒ :/ to holþe hire in folie
50 Wiþoute spoushoþe his leman :/ in forme of lecherie
¶ Þo þis maiþe þis ifeʒ :/ louþe heo gan to crie
Louerd heo seiþe ic biþe þe :/ þt ibore were of marie
Anþ for to bringe ous out of wo :/ beiþeft on þe treo
Wite mi boþi in clenniffe :/ þt hit iwõmib ne beo
55 Boþi ʒt soule ic þe bitake :/ for þane beþ ic ifeo
Biset ic am wiþ liþere men :/ þt ynemai noʒt fleo

E

Louerd ȝef me stodefast herte :/ þane beþ to afonge
þᵗ ich fram þe ne fleahi noȝt :/ for none tourmentz stronge
¶ Seite margarete was forþ ibroȝt :/ tofore þe liþere iustise
60 þᵗ þoȝte of hire his wille habbe :/ in folie in alle wise
He bihuld þis maide faste :/ damaisele he sede
Tel me of wham þu ert icome :/ ⁊ of what cunrede
¶ þis maide hī ȝaf ansuare anon :/ wiþoute eni brede
tel me ek what is þi name :/ ⁊ what lyf þu bost lede
65 Mi cunrede he seide is couþ :/ hit ne mai noȝt beo ihud
Mi fader is gret man ynouȝ :/ among ȝou her icud
terbose þᵗ þe heȝifte maifter :/ of ȝoure temple is
þu axest ek what is mi name :/ margarete iwis
þᵗ is ⁊ was mi furste name :/ an heȝere name iᶜ nom
70 ⁊ criftene wōman iᶜ wole beo iclepeþ :/ for mi cristendom
For þᵗ is myn heȝifte name :/ þerof mest iᶜ telle
For on ihū crist iᶜ bileoue :/ ⁊ forsake hī neuer ynelle
¶ Þo Olibrius ihurde þis :/ he was alout of rede
As he wer in anoþer worðle :/ hende maide he sede
75 Þis tuo þinges þᵗ þu nemnedeft erft :/ bicomeþ þe faire ⁊ suete
þᵗ þu beo icome of heȝe blode :/ ⁊ þᵗ þu hote margarete
Þuse tuo bicomeþ þe wel ynouȝ :/ suche maide noble ⁊ freo
¶ Ac þe þridde bicomeþ þe noȝt :/ as þu miȝt iseo
þᵗ þu onoure þe false god :/ þe gywes honge on þe treo
80 Such noble maide as þu ert :/ god schulde þᵗ þu ne beo
For such hende bodi as þu bereft :/ bicome bet in bowre
In myn armes to clippe ⁊ cuffe :/ þan such a fals god to onoure
þᵗ maide hī ȝaf ansuare anon :/ mid wel mylde mode
Sire heo seide þᵗ þe gywes :/ honge god on rode
85 For hire liþere dede hi beoþ :/ in þe pyne of helle ibroȝt
Ac naþeles hi dude ous god :/ þeȝ hi ne louede ous noȝt
For we were out of pyne :/ þurf his deþ ibroȝt
Ac hi þᵗ hī þerto broȝte :/ nabbe noȝt so iþoȝt
Þo gan Olibrius for wraþþe :/ loude crie ⁊ grede
90 He let nyme þis holi maide :/ ⁊ into strong prifoun lede

þt so beoþe was ⁊ burk :' þt mon miȝte agrife
And wende to his falfe godes :' to do sacrifife
f. 86 Amorwe he let clipie knyȝtes :' of þe lawe grete ⁊ wife
⁊ sette hī silue amidde hē alle :' as an heȝ juftife
95 And lette fetche þis holi maide :' to afonge hire dom
Bifore þis tratours mylbeliche :' þis holi maide com
⁊ makede þe signe of þe croiz :' ⁊ to our louerd al hire nom
⁊ al preft was for his loue :' to afonge criftendom
¶ Olibrius wel fawe spac :' ⁊ seide margarete
100 Vnderftond þi noblei :' hou gent þu ert ⁊ suete
And reu on þi faire bodi :' þt þu hit nepere noȝt
For ic hopie þt þu haft :' to niȝt þe bet biþoȝt
Chus weþer þu wold mid schindiffe :' to deþe beon ibroȝt
Oþer honoury our godes :' þt alle þing habbeþ iwroȝt
¶ Sire quaþ þis holi maide :' oure louerd hī silf tok
Strong deþ to bringe ous out of pyne :' ⁊ wordles ioye forsok
For hī ic wole þane deþ afonge :' ynabbe þerof no doute
Raþer þan to abowe adoun myn heued :' ȝoure false godes to
¶ Þo he furde as he witles were :' þe schrewe juftife   [aloute
110 So grisliche he clipede his tourmentours :' þt men miȝte agrife
Nymeþ he seide þis hore anon :' ⁊ hongeþ hire on a treo
⁊ todraweþ hire so fel ⁊ flefch :' þt me hire guttes ifeo
Al naked byndeþ hire fafte :' þt heo nowhar ne fleo
þt of hire schendful dede :' oure godes awreke beo
¶ Þe tourmentours wel ȝare were :' to vuel here hurte brouȝ
Þe maide hi stripde naked sone :' ⁊ bounden hire fafte ynouȝ
Al fram þe vrþe hihongen hire up :' ⁊ leiden hire to grounde
Wiþ scurgen ⁊ wiþ kene precken :' hi makeden hire meni wonde
Al hi to drowe hire tendre flefch :' þt reuþ hit is to telle
120 Bi stremes þt blod orn adoun :' so water doþ of welle
For hire lymes tendre were :' þe scourgen smerte ⁊ kene
Bi peces þe flesch orn adoun :' þe bones were ifene
¶ Allas hire suete tendre flesch :' so filliche todrawe was so
Allas hou miȝte eni man :' for reuþe such dede do

125 Wiþ oules hi browe hire wombe :/ þe gottes ifene were
¶ Allas also þe schynbful bebe :/ hire binne lymes hi totere
  Þe juftife for schynbiffe :/ nolbe loke þerto
  Ac bihulb abac ⁊ tournbe his ezen :/ ⁊ meni oþer also
  Þe men þᵗ stobe in þe place :/ ⁊ al þe bebe ifeʒe
130 Hi makebe beol ⁊ sorewe ynouʒ :/ ⁊ wepe mib here eʒe
  Maibe hi seibe margarete :/ so gent þu were ⁊ henbe
  Haue ruþe of þi faire bobi :/ þᵗ me ne lete hit noʒt þus to renbe
  For þe worþ ʒut wel ynouʒ :/ ⁊ þu wole þi þoʒt wenbe
  Þᵗ maibe cafte op hire eʒe :/ ⁊ anfuerebe attan enbe
135 Anb seibe ʒe wickebe consaillers :/ goþ fram me anon
  Anoþer consail ich haue itake :/ ich forsake ʒou echon
  Olibrius sat ⁊ bihulb :/ hou hure lymes yrne ablobe
  Heo ne miʒte hit for beol ifeo :/ ne meni oþer þᵗ þer stobe
  Wiþ his mantel for ruþe ⁊ beol :/ he helebe boþe his eʒe
140 So bube meni anoþer ek :/ þᵗ hi þe beol ne seʒe
  Maibe seibe Olibrius :/ tourn þi þoʒt iᶜ rebe
  ⁊ among alle wȳmen þᵗ ich iknowe :/ befc þi lyf þu schalt lebe
  Beo stille quaþ þis holi maibe :/ þu liþere þing beo stille
  Þu haft poer ouer mi bobi :/ for to bo þi wille
145 Ac mi louerb witeþ mi soule wel :/ þᵗ þu hir noʒt ne spille
  For þu ne miʒt mib al þi miʒte :/ anuʒe hire worþ a fille
¶ Þo þe liþere ifeʒ :/ þᵗ he nemiʒte noʒt spebe
  He nemiʒte for beol ifeo hire :/ so beolfulliche blebe
  He makebe he bileue here tourmentours :/ ⁊ to prifoun hire lebe
150 Forte hi wifte what bo wiþ hire :/ as hi nome to rebe
¶ Þis maibe lai in prifoun strong :/ aleling alone
  Heo nufte of hire wounbe :/ to wham makie hire mone
  Bote Angles confortebe hire :/ ⁊ aboun to hire aliʒte
  Heo was fafte in oreisons :/ bi baye ⁊ bi nyʒte
155 Our louerb he bab for his grace :/ þᵗ he senbe hire sum siʒte
  Of þe beuel þᵗ werrebe hire :/ ⁊ which was his miʒte
  Me telleþ þᵗ þe beuel com :/ to þis maibe swye
  In aforme of abragoun :/ ac ynot whar hi lye

He ȝenebe 'ɫ gan his ouere cheoke :/ ouer hire heueb bo
160 'ɫ his nyþere cheoke :/ byneþe at hire ho
'ɫ forſualȝ so þis maibe :/ he yenebe er wel wibe   [abibe
Heo wenbe into a sori wombe :/ ac heo nolbe þer noȝt longe
For þe signe heo makebe of þe croiz :/ þe beuel toberſte anon
'ɫ þis maibe hol 'ɫ sounb :/ out of þe worm gan gon
165 Ac þis ne telle i^c noȝt forsoþe :/ for hit nis noȝt to soþe iwrite
Ac weþer hit is soþ oþer hit nis :/ ynot noman þ^t wite
Ac aȝe cunbe hit wer þ^t þe beuel :/ were to beþe ibroȝt
For henemai þolie nanne beþ :/ ynemai hit ileoue noȝt
¶ Also yneleoue hit noȝt :/ þ^t his miȝtes were so stronge
170 Eni so holi creatoure :/ in his wombe afonge
Ac forsoþe hit is iwrite :/ þ^t in manes like
Þis beuel to þis maibe com :/ 'ɫ fonbebe hir to swike
Anon so he to þis maibe com :/ hire to confonbe
Þis maibe aros wel balbeliche :/ 'ɫ nom hī bi þe honbe
175 Þu haſt he seibe ynou ibo :/ þu ne schalt nomore
Anon þu schalt to stope :/ for þi false lore
f. 87 He nom bi his liþere pol :/ 'ɫ harbe hī to grunbe caſte
Anb hire riȝt fot anon he sette :/ vpe his necke bihynbe faſte
Þu beuel heo seibe þat ert so strong :/ ful of prute 'ɫ onbe
180 Þe were betere habbe bileueb atom :/ þan icome me to fonbe
Li boun þu ert ouercome :/ i^c wole on þe stonbe
Þu miȝt telle atom hou þu were :/ vnber a maibenes honbe
Faſte heo bonb þis foule wiȝt :/ 'ɫ scourgebe hī sore
Grisliche he seibe :/ henbe maibe þin ore
185 Allas þ^t i^c here com :/ me miȝte is her me bynome
Allas þ^t atenbre maibe :/ me haþ þus ouercome
If hit were aman of mi strenȝþe :/ iwis me nere noȝt
Ac ischenb i^c am þ^t amaibe :/ me haþ to grounbe ibroȝt
Maibe for þin henbeschipe :/ þu haue merci of me
190 Let me go at þis tyme :/ yneschal neuereſt bere þe
Ich bibbe for þi kynnes loue :/ þ^t beoþ myne freonb echone
'ɫ serueþ me as þu woſt :/ alle wel bote þu one

¶ A þeof quaþ þis holi maibe :/ ȝut þu schalt abibe
Þu schalt telle me of ȝoure art :/ þt fleoþ aboute so wibe
195 Whi werrie ȝe cristene men :/ among alle oþere mest
Sertes maibe quaþ þe beuel :/ for hi serueþ ous left
˜t mest schame ous boþ of alle men :/ ˜t mest beoþ oure fon
Anb mest strenȝþe habbeþ of here gob :/ among ous to gon
˜t ech man mai bi riȝte cunbe :/ fonbi his fon to schenbe
200 ˜t þane ne beo we noȝt to blame :/ to bo on oure enbe
Among men of þe olbe lawe :/ we furbe while so
Anb seruebe wel here heȝe gob :/ ˜t we habbe enuye þerto
¶ Þo com salamon þe kyng :/ þt was of þe lawe
˜t seruebe wel al miȝti gob :/ ˜t to his seruise gan brawe
205 Þerfore we habbe enuye þerto :/ ˜t fonbebe wel faste
Ac his louerb hi ȝaf such poer :/ þt he ous ouercom atte laste
˜t in a strong vetles ous broȝte :/ ˜t in a put ous caste
˜t makebe ous þerinne faste ynouȝ :/ ˜t siþþe atfore hit butte
Þe while þt he aliue was :/ we nabbe poer non
210 Þe while we were so faste ibut :/ among men to gon
Ne after his beþ noþemo :/ if men he silf hit nolbe
Ac men ous broȝte þerof siþþe :/ for couetise of golbe
For as we were þerinne ibut :/ we gonne blowe ˜t blaste
˜t briȝt fur glowinge reb :/ out of þe vrþe caste ·
215 Þer come men wel ofte forþ :/ ˜t þis fur iseȝe þere
˜t seibe hit ne miȝte noȝt beo :/ bote þer gret t[r]esour were
Lo hou reb come þerout þe breþ :/ loke we anon
˜t we worþeþ riche ynouȝ :/ of rebe golbe echon
Ho bulue ˜t fonbe þe vetles :/ þt we were on iput
220 Her hi seibe we habbeþ ifonbe :/ þe tresour is her ibut
Þis vetles hi breke anon :/ ˜t wenbe wel to catche
˜t fonbe tresour feble inouȝ :/ atte furste hatche
To here behoue feble ynouȝ :/ ˜t to oþere also
For we were glab ynouȝ :/ þo we were of prisoun ibo
225 ˜t wenbe ˜t fulbe al þeir abowe :/ alþus in eche sibe
We wenbeþ ˜t berieþ men þus :/ in þe lonbe wibe

Nou ıc þe habbe margarete :/ ıtolþ of al our beþe
Haue ruþe ıc bıbbe þe :/ ꝥ brıng me of þıs wrechheþe
ꝥ þench þt maıþenes scholþe beo :/ ful of mılce ꝥ ore
230 Ich bıhote þe ynelle :/ neuerefꞇ þe berıe more
¶ Aꞇꞇe lasꞇe þıs holı maıþe :/ þıs foule þıng leꞇ wenþe
Þe schrewe was þo glaþ ynouȝ :/ þo he was ouꞇ of benþe
¶ Þe ıufꞇıse anoþer daı :/ ın hıs sıge hī seꞇꞇe
ꝥ þıs holı maıþe margarete :/ bıfore hī me feꞇꞇe
235 ꝥ eschꞇe whar hıre wılle were :/ þe ȝuꞇ ꞇo ꞇournıe hıre þoȝꞇ
Serꞇes sıre quaþ þıs maıþe :/ þu speyꞇ aboute noȝꞇ
¶ Þıs ıufꞇıse þo ın grete wraþþe :/ leꞇ makıe afur fafꞇe
ꝥ leꞇ strıpe þıs holı maıþe al nakeþ :/ ꝥ amıþþe hıre cafꞇe
Ac þe fur aqueynꞇe sone :/ ꝥ ne mıȝꞇe hıre berne noȝꞇ
240 Al hol ꝥ sound heo was efꞇ :/ ꞇofore þe ıufꞇıfe ıbroȝꞇ [bounþe
Þer was wreþþe ꝥ sorewe ynouȝ :/ hıre feꞇ ꝥ honþe behynþe hı
ꝥ cafꞇe hıre ın a wel þeope waꞇer :/ hıre heueþ ꞇowarþ þe grounþe
Ac our louerþes myȝꞇe ıs moche :/ hıre benþes ꞇo berfꞇe anon
ꝥ al harmles heo com sofꞇe :/ ouꞇ of þe waꞇer gon
¶ Þıs ıufꞇıfe was neȝ ouꞇ of wıꞇꞇe :/ þo he hurþe þıs ꞇıþınge
Cerꞇes he seıþe ın some manere :/ we schulle ꞇo þeþe þe brınge
He leꞇ heꞇe waꞇer oð seoþınge :/ ꝥ þo hıꞇ boıllebe fafꞇe
He leꞇ nyme þıs holı maıþe :/ ꝥ þer amıþþe hıre cafꞇe
¶ Þo heo was þerınne ıþo :/ þe vrþe quakeþe anon
250 Suyþe grıslıche abouꞇe :/ þt þaꞇ folc brabþe echon
¶ Þt maıþe ȝeoþe ouꞇ of þe waꞇer :/ þo hıꞇ seoþınge was
Among al þt folc :/ þt no þe wors hıre nas
¶ Louerþ moche ıs þı mıȝꞇe :/ as me maı albaı ıseo
Þt enı þıng ın such ꞇourmenꞇ :/ alyue mıȝꞇe beo
255 Vyf þousenþ ın þe place :/ þo hı þt ıseȝe
ꞇournþe anon ꞇo crıfꞇenþom :/ ꝥ hereþe oure louerþ heȝe
¶ Þo þe ıufꞇıfe þt ıseȝ :/ he gan ꞇo greþe ꝥ grone
He nom þıs men þt ꞇournþe so :/ ꝥ smoꞇ of hıre heueþes echone
ꝥ leꞇ nyme ek þıs holı maıþe :/ ꝥ smyꞇe of hıre heueþ also
260 Þt heo were ıbroȝꞇ of lyue :/ ꝥ be ouꞇ of wo

f. 88 Itake heo was amanqueller :/ malcus was his name
He fonde hou he miȝte lede :/ þis maide mid mest schame
He ladde hire wiþoute þe toun :/ þer me boþ of bawe
Þeoues ⁊ eke oþer men :/ idampned þurf þe lawe
¶ Þo margarete was ibroȝt :/ to þis vile stede
Heo bad þe quellere ȝeue hire furst :/ to bidde hire bede
So þᵗ malcus ȝaf hire furst :/ ⁊ bad hire hiȝie faste
Þis holi maide sat akneo :/ ⁊ hire eȝen to heuene caste
Louerd heo seide ihū crist :/ þᵗ bouȝtest me on þe rode
270 Mid mouþ ⁊ hurte iᶜ þonki þe :/ ⁊ wel auȝte of alle gode
Þᵗ þi wille is to bringe me :/ out of þis wordles wrechhede
⁊ wiþoute wem of mi bodi :/ to þe ioye of heuene lede
Grante me iᶜ bidde þe :/ for þi wonden fyue
Þᵗ if eni man haþ munde :/ louerd of me lyue
275 ⁊ of þe pyne þᵗ ich habbe ipoled :/ louerd for þi grace
Oþer wryt in god entente :/ oþer ret in eni place
If hi biddeþ in god entente :/ grante hē milce ⁊ ore
If eny in anuy beoþ :/ bring hē out of sore
If eni man in honour of me :/ eni chapel doþ rere
280 Oþer eni weued in churche :/ oþer eni liȝt fyndeþ þere
In honour of me vpe his coust :/ louerd bidde iᶜ þe
If hi biddeþ þing þᵗ is to bidde :/ grante hē for loue of me
And if eni wōman clipeþ to me :/ in trauail of childe
Oþer before hire mi lyf me rede :/ louerd beo hire mylde
285 Ne let hire noȝt þerwiþ spille :/ ac bring þᵗ child to siȝte
⁊ al sauf of his moder wombe :/ mid alle his lymes riȝte
Moder ⁊ child saue hē :/ louerd for loue of me
Louerd for þi moder loue :/ þᵗ þis bone igranted beo
¶ Anon so þis maide :/ þis bone habbe ido
290 Þer com a þondre suyþe strong :/ ⁊ liȝtinge
Þᵗ þe folc þᵗ stod þeraboute :/ ful adoun for drede
⁊ seye þer as hi were astoned :/ ⁊ as hi were dede
¶ A coluere whitere þan eni snow :/ fram heuene liȝte adoun
In þe þondre to þᵗ maide :/ after hire oreisoun

295 Maide hit seide margarete :/ iblesced þuert 't hende
    Our louerd granteþ þe þi bone :/ to þe worldes ende
    Com nou to reste for oure louerd :/ after þe boþ sende
    Þu schalt after þi stronge pyne :/ to þe ioye of heuene wende
  ¶ Þis colure to heuene aȝe :/ fleȝ as heo com
300 Þis maide aros wel mylbeliche :/ to fonge hir martirdom
    Malcus heo seide com nou forþ : 't þi louerdes heste do
    For nou in ini louerdes name :/ prest i^c am þerto
    To margarete merci :/ þis manqueller sede
    I ne þerfte for al þe worlde :/ do such a fol dede
305 So moche liȝt aboute þe i^c iseo :/ of heuene in eche ende
    Ac i^c wole wiþ þe deye :/ 't wiþ þe þider wende
  ¶ Malcus seide þis holi maide :/ bote þu do þis dede
    Ne tyt þe no part wiþ me :/ þerfore do i^c rede
  ¶ Þis malcus brouȝ þo his swerd :/ swete louerd he sede
310 Þis dulful dede forȝif þu me :/ for i^c hit do for drede
  ¶ Þis holi heued he smot of :/ anon so he habbe ibo
    In hir riȝt half he ful adoun :/ 't deide wiþ hire also
    Riȝt as þ^t maide deide :/ as al þ^t folc iseȝ
    A whyt coluere þer fleȝ of hire :/ into heuene anheȝ
315 In þisse manere þis holi maide :/ hir lyf to ende brouȝte
    Of gret vertu is hire lyf :/ ho so þeron þoȝte
    Wȳman þ^t wiþ oþere whan hi childerne bere
    Hit were god þ^t hi rabbe hire lyf :/ þe sikerer hi were
  ¶ Nou seinte margarete þ^t holi maide we biddeþ attan ende
320 þ^t heo bidde for ous þ^t we mote :/ to þe ioye of heuene wende.

MEIDAN MAREGRETE.

MS. Trin. Coll. Cantab.
Hickes, vol. i. p. 224.

1 Olde ant yonge i prei ou oure folief for to lete.
Denchet on god þat yef ou wit oure funnef to bete.
Here i mai tellen ou. wid wordef feire ant fwete.
De vie of one meidan. waf hoten Maregrete.
2 Hire faber waf a patriac. af ic ou tellen may.
In auntioge wif echef i ðe falfe lay.
Deve godef ant doumbe. he ferved nitt ant day.
So beden mony opere. þat finget weilawey.
3 Theobofius waf if nome. on crift ne levede he noutt.
He levede on þe falfe godef. ðat peren wid honden wroutt.
Do þat child fculde chriftine ben. it com him well in þoutt.
E bed wen it were ibore. to beþe it were ibnoutt.
4 De moder waf an heþene wif. þat hire to wyman bere.
Do þat child ibore waf. nolde ho hit furfare.
Ho fende it into afye. wid meffagerf ful yare.
To a norice þat hire wifte. ant fette hire to lore.
5 De norice þat hire wifte. children aheuede feuene.
De eitteþe waf maregrete. criftef may of heuene.
Talef ho ani tolde. ful feire ant ful euene.
Wou ho þoleden martirdom. fein Laurence ant feinte Steuene.
6 De norice hire fedde. wid wel muchele wunne.
Alle loueden hire. in þe toun þer ho waf inne.
Ho toc hire to ihū chrift. ant leuede al hire cunne.
Do ho couþe of wifdom. ho hatede muche funne.

7 Sone fo þe maiban waf of þrettene winter elbe.
Þo wifte hire norice fcep. baief 1 þe felbe.
Þir felawef þat hire bifeten. ful yerne hire bihulbe.
Wou ho makebe ir bone. to ihū þat al mai welbe.
8 Olibriuf waf louerb. afe þe boc uf telle.
Þe haueb auntioȝe. to yeuen ant to felle.
Þe feruebe nitt ant bay. fenbef in helle.
Alle þat leueben on ihū chrift. e heitt hem aquelle.
9 From afie to auntioge. bet milef tene ant fiue.
Foŋ to flen chriftene men. he hiebe him biliue.
E fei maiben Maregrete. fcep biforen hire briue.
Sone wolbe þe farezin. habben hire to wiue.
10 Þe faib to hif ferjaunf. a maiban ic ifee.
Faret fomme of myne men. ant fatchet hire to me.
Bi my lay yef ho if boren. of cunnraben free.
Oꝭ all hire cunne. beft fcal hire bee.
11 Ant for ir feirneffe. þan ho bee comen oꝭ þrelle.
Þire weblac ne fcal ho nout lefen all.
Ful wel ic fcal ir cloþen. wib ciclatoun ant pelle.
Þo fcal be my leuemon. fo me hire fcal calle.
12 Ðe fergaunz eben afe he am beb. to meiban Maregrete.
Af a wift ir norice fcep. nout fer from þe ftrete.
Sone muchele a hire boben. ant more a hire bihete.
Ðe trouþe oꝭ hire herte. nolbe ho nout furlete.
13 Ðe fergaunz beben ar ernbe. feire ant fele fiþe.
Meiban Maregrete nulle we nout mitte fike.
Olibriuf if louerb. of auntioȝe þe riche.
Þe wil het þe to wiue. wel it may þe like.
14 Maiban Maregrete. britt fo eni leme.
Sone ham onfwerebe. wib wel milbe fteuene.
Ic abbe iyeuen my maibanhob. ihū chrift of heuene.
Þe me wite to bay. for if nomen feuene.
15 Ihū chrift my louerb. ðat beet þolebe for uf alle.
Ðe heie king of heuene. to him wol ic calle.

Of mine ftable herte. ne lete ir neuer at falle.
Ne lete neuere my bodi. to bai in funne falle.
16 Ihū chrift mi louerd. to þe ic wile me yelde.
Þou neuebeft bigunne. ne neuer neuebeft ende.
Yef þi wille were. þe holi goft þou me fende.
Dat from þe farefinz. i mitte me defende.
17 Al my cun i furfake. to þe niþe cne.
Ihū chrift my louerd. to þe i take me.
For þi loue here. martir woll i bee.
Def houndef habbet me bifet. ne mai ic henne fle.
18 De fargaunz ayein eden. ant feiben here fawe.
Of alle þine mitte. ne yened ho word ati hawe.
Of all þat we faiden. al ir þunchet plawe.
Þo leuet on ihū chrift. to waraunt ho him drawet.
19 Denne fpec olibriuf. awarie him fonne ant mone.
Of alle mine fergaunf. gode nabbi none,
Bringet hire bifore me. ic turne hir mod ful fone.
Þo fcal leuen o mine godef. er halfuey to none.
20 De fergaunz ayein eden. ant cumen hire imete.
Þo leiden honden hire upon. ant ledden ir to þe ftrete.
Þo com biforn Olibriuf. ant he hire con grete.
Þe asked what ir nome waf. ho feide Maregrete.
21 Meidan Maregret. my leuemon þou fcal bee.
Ant habben þe to wive. yef þu art of cunne fre.
Yef þou art of þnellef. ic yeue þe gold ant fee.
Dou fcalt be my leuemon. fo long so ic be.
22 De meidan him onfwerede. fwiþe feire anon.
Chriftine wiman ic am. iheuen of þe fonfton.
Ihū chrift my louerd. to him ic wille gon.
I nule leten if loue. for oþer neuer on.
23 Leueftou on ihū chrift. men beden him o rode.
Yef þou leueft þat e leuet. ic holde þe for wode.
Or if fide orn adoun. þe water ant te blode.
De croune waf of þornef. þat on if heued ftode.

MEIDAN MAREGRETE. 37

24 Đe meiðan him anſwereðe. aſe þe anȝel hire kenðe.
　Ye beðen him on roðe. al chriſtine folc ta menðe.
　Ant ſeþen in to helle. þe holi goſt he ſenðe.
　To aleſen chriſtine men. ant þiðer þou ſcalt wenðe.
25 Ðo iſei þe fareſin. þat him ueſ no bot.
　To ſtriuen wið þat meiðan. ir herte waſ ſo goð.
　Ƕe beð þat ho bounðen hire. boþen honð ant fot.
　Anð ðepe into priſun ðon. turneð e wolðe ir moð.
26 Meiðan Maregret. one nitt in priſun lai.
　Ƕo com biforn olibriuſ. on þat oþer ðai.
　Meiðan Maregrete. lef up on my lay.
　Ant ihū þat tou leueſt on. þou bo him al awey.
27 Lef on me ant be my wif. ful wel þe mai ſpeðe.
　Auntioge ant aſie. ſcaltou han to meðe.
　Ciclatoun ant purpel pal. ſcaltou haue to weðe.
　Wið alle þe meteſ of my lonð. ful wel i ſcal þe feðe.
28 Alle þine reðeſ. i ðo ut of my þoutt.
　Ant take me to ihū chriſt. þat me haueð iwrott.
　For he all þiſ miððelerð. makeðe of rett noutt.
　Anð ȝeþen mið if ſwete fleſc. of helle he uſ boutt.
29 Ðenne ſpec olibriuſ. nou it ſcal ben ſene.
　Upon wam þou leueſt. ant wi þou art ſo kene.
　Ƕonget ir up bi þe fet. hire louerð to tene.
　Wið ſcourgeſ betet hire fleiſc. þat ho ir beet wene.
30 Ðe fergaunz beðen þat he beð. on hire gunne ſtriue.
　Wið ſwopen ant wið ſcourgeſ. boþe ful riue.
　Ðe bloð ron of hire fleiſc. wnðerliche ſwiþe.
　Alle ho wenðen. þat broutt a were of liue.
31 Ðo ſpec olibriuſ. bi hire þer he ſtoð.
　Meiðan Maregrete. iſ þiſ pine goð.
　Lef nou on my goðeſ. ant ſone wenð ti moð.
　Ƕaue merci of þi fleiſc. me ſpillet þi bloð.
32 Ihū chriſt my louerð. waſ born me beðlehem.
　On þe holi meiðan. he ſenðe litt ant glem.

Þou beſt aſe [þe] techet. ſatanaſ þin em.
Me þenchet þeſ pine ſwete. ſo em milc rem.
33 Do ſpec olibriuſ. nauet ho none care.
Of al þilke pine. al ir þunchet plawe.
Wiþ oure ſcarp naileſ. ir hube al to brawe.
Aſe clene from þe fleiſc. ſo hounb it hebe ignawe.
34 Þe ſergaunz beben ſo. to hire gonnen go.
Al þet ſel from þe fleiſc. gunnen ho to flo.
Al þet blob þat in hire waſ out it ebe þo.
Al þiſ ho þolebe. ant oþere pinen mo.
35 Summe þat ter ſtoben. ar herte waſ ful ſore.
For hire wite fleiſc. ant for ir yelewe here.
Maiban Maregrete. of þe we habbet care.
Leſ on him ant be hiſ wiſ. ne þoele þou ſo nan more.
36 Awei ye euele confilerſ. wi ſaib ye ſo.
Mit ſwopeſ ant mit ſcorgeſ. habbe ye me flo.
Ihū chriſteſ angleſ. comet me to ant ſro.
Al þiſ iſ my ioie. ne bo ye me ſo wo.
37 Denne ſpec olibriuſ. Þiſ iſ oure pouſte.
Er hauebeſtou eyen. nou maiſtou nout iſee.
Leſ on me ant be my wiſ. ful wel i rebe þe.
Yeſ þou leueſt oþer weiſ. ſclawen ſcaltou bee.
38 De gobeſ þat tou leueſt on. are bebe aſe a ſton.
Of my louerbeſ ioie. ne mai tellen no mon.
Nou þou haueſt pouſte. of my fleiſce ant bon.
To beruen myne ſoule. pouſte naueſtou non.
39 Olibriuſ heiſt. þat mai in priſun bon.
De holi goſt from heuene. to hire com ful ſon.
Ant þe robe in hiſ honb. þat chriſt waſ on ibon.
Ant ſcon aſe britt. ſo ſonne abouten none.
40 Meiban Maregrete. ne brebe þou nowib.
Di ſege iſ makeb in heuene. biforen ihū ful britt.
Niſ no tonge an erþe. ne non eyen litt.
Þat mai telle þe ioie. þat waſ maket of þe to nitt.

41 Meiban Maregrete. britt so eny leme.
Iblesset wort þou to bai. of al þat i con neme.
De heie king of heuene. ful wel hauet herbe þi steuene.
Þe þe senbe þis crois. þine fon to aferene.
42 Blessed be ihū christ. þat me bote sende.
Ant if holi angel. to me þat he wende.
Fader ant sone ant holi gost. þat alle us mai amende.
Ne lete neuer to bai. myne herte wende.
43 Meiban Maregrete. lokede hire bi side.
Þo sei a foul bragun. ine þe hurne glide.
Berninde ase fur. ant goninde ful wide.
Þo wert ase grene. so gres ine someres tide.
44 De fur flei of is mouþe. so leie of brenston.
Þo fel to þen erþe. ant quakede uich bon.
Þe nom ir in is mouþe. ant swalen hire anon.
Þe barst a two peces. felawe nauede he non.
45 Meiban Maregrete. upon þe bragun stod.
Bliþe was ir herte. ioiful was ir mod.
Sclawen was þe bragun. þoru þe uertu of þe rod.
Blessed be ihū christ. is mitten is so god.
46 Meiban Maregret. þe bragun ede fro.
Þo sei anoþer beuel. þer inne þo.
E heuede eien on is cleu. ant eken on is to.
Ne mitte foulore þinȝ. neuer erþe go.
47 Þo wende to þe loþe þing. þe robe in hire hond.
Doru þe mitte of ihū christ. wid her wempel ho hin bond.
Þo toc him bi þe toppe. abouten ho him swong.
Sette ir fot in is necke. ant to þen erþe wrong.
48 Sai me nouþe wat tou art. þou foule loþe þinȝ.
Upon wam þou bileuest. ant wa is þi kinȝ.
Ant wo þe hider sende. to maken stourbing.
Tel me nou swiþe. ant into helle spring.
49 Leuedi for þe rode loue. þat is i þine honde.
Þef up þi fot a littel. þat ine myn necke stond.

Muchel ic habbe iwalken. bi water ant bi londe.
Naſ ic neuer ibounden. in ſo harde bonde.
50 Ruffin waſ my broþer. þat tou here ſclowe.
De wile e waſ aliue. e couþe ſunneſ inowe.
E bebe men to ſunne. þere fore we loude lowe.
Ant yeld here ſeruiſe. ofte mid muchele wowe.
51 In a dragoneſ hche. i ſende him to þe.
To turne þine herte. ant apaie me.
De if iborſten a two. ibounden haueſtou me.
A maidain hauet uſ ouercomen. noutt niſ oure pouſte.
52 Belſebug if my nome. i ne may þe nout lie.
Ne mai ic longe þolien. þe pine þat i drie.
Al ic wolde biſwike. þat iſen mitte mid eie.
Nab ic none mitte. þe nou to ſtraye.
53 Wen ic wiſt a wif. ſculde be bet of berne.
Ic com þider ſone. ſwift aſ an erne.
Ant wen i þider come. to croke fot oþer arme.
Ant te wif ir ſelue. i fonde to furfarne.
54 Daue þi paiſ þou foule þing. þou fli into helle.
Ne be þou ſo hardi. lengore þat tou duelle.
I bidde ihū chriſt. þi mitte þat he felle.
Dou fal into helle. ſo ſton beet into welle.
55 Upon þet oþer dai. alute beforn non.
Olibriuſ heitte þe mai. ut of priſun don.
De ſergaunz were ſnelle. ant broutten hire ſon.
Wid þe rode on hire honde. þat chriſt waſ on idon.
56 Do ſpec olibriuſ. i wiſ e waſ ful wroet.
Ant ſaide to if ſergaunz. wonder wou ho goet.
Lef on me Maregrete. ant haue mete ant cloet.
Do after me ant be my wif. ne be þe þi lif ſo loet.
57 Awarieð worþe þine godeſ. þat tou leueſt inne.
Do weren yare awarieð. ant al ful of ſunne.
Do beet al of helle. of ſatanaſ cunne.
Wene þou weneſt beſt to liue. to him awoller þe winne.

MEIDAN MAREGRETE.

58 Ac bo nou wel ant lef on him. þat mabe þe to mon.
    Faber ant fone ant holi goft. þat þif worlb bigon.
    Ant let þe folewen. in holi fonfton.
    Afe ihū chrift waf ymfelf. y þe flem iurban.
59 Đenne fpec olibriuf. a pine ic chulle kenne.
    Wellinbe laumpef. letet on hire renne.
    From þe necke to þe to. fcalben ir af an henne.
    Bote ho turne hire mob. to beþe ye fculen ir brenne.
60 Đe fergaunz beben al fo. ely letten ho welle.
    Þeie upon ir heuebe. wallinbe letten ho felle.
    It orn on hire wite fleifc. fo water bet of welle.
    Đe holi goft ir wift. ne mitten ho hire aquelle.
61 Alle weren þe farefinz. fo boc if writen wib enke.
    To bringen hire of liue. ho gunnen hem biþenke.
    In a fet ful of water. ho gunnen hire abrencke.
    Ant bote ho turne hire mob. þer a fcal abrencke.
62 Louerb yef þi wille if. a water ic ifee.
    Drin ic chulle beien. for þe loue of þe.
    Đet fet bigon to berften. þe folc bigon to fle.
    Đe engel ir nom of þe water. þat alle it mitten ifee.
63 Đer bileueben on ihū chrift. a þoufend ant fiue.
    Al wibouten chilbren. ant wibouten wiue.
    To bon ham to beþe. he hiebe bileue.
    For ho leueben on ihū chrift. he broutte hem of liue.
64 Wel fey þe farezin. ne mitte hire bere.
    E clepeb forb malcuf. if monquellere.
    Þe beb leben hire wiboute toun. oþer hire bere.
    Ant bringen hire of liue. wib fworbe oþer wib fpere.
65 Do ho com wibout þe toun. þer me ir fculbe fclo.
    Al fiwebe hire. þat euer mitte go.
    Đe winb begun to blowen. þe fonne wert al blo.
    Đet folc fel to þen erþe. ne wiften ho hire nout þo.
66 Ure lorb fenbe to hire. a ful feire fteuene.
    Ant gon hire greten. ful feire ant wel euene.

Bleffeð be þou ðai. með al þat ic con nemme.
To ðay þou fcalt ben icrounet. biforn þe king of heuene.
67 Malchuſ herðe þeſ worðeſ. he fette him acne.
Meiðan Maregrete. þi louerð hat fpeke wið þe.
Ant a þoufent angleſ. aboute þe ifee.
Spreð þin houð. ant nym my fwerðe. ant haue merci of me.
68 Ðo fpec þat meiðan. feinte Maregrete.
Broþer yef þi wil iſ. abið alutel yet.
Ðe wile i make my bone. to him þat may bete.
Biðbe wat tou euer wile. ic it wole gete.
69 Alle þat my liſ. wollet heren oþer reðe.
Oþer for me cirche fette. með almeſ ðeðe.
Ihū chriſt my louerð. mit monfcipe þou am feðe.
Ðe heie bliſſe of hiuene. haþben ho to meðe.
70 Alle þat habbet me aðay. ine memorie.
Oþer mið goðe herte. iheret myne vie.
Ihū chriſt my louerð. fone [o] fainte Marie.
Þaue merci of þe fouleſ. leie were þe boneſ lye.
71 Ihū chriſt my louerð. wen wimman bet fcal be.
Iher here bone. yef ho clepet to me.
Deliure hir myð menske. for þe loue of þe tre.
Ðat tou ðeðeſt þi boði on. to maken uſ alle fre.
72 Ðo fpec ure louerð. feinte Marie fone.
Bi heuene bi erþe. bi fonne bi mone.
Maiðan Maregrete. i cuiþe þe þi bone.
Cum into þe ioie. þer þou fcalt euer wone.
73 Maiðan Maregrete. ir bone haueðe þenne.
Malcuſ fmit of myne heueð. furyeuen iſ þe þe funne.
Ðat ne ðuðe ic nout. for al þiſ worlðeſ wune.
Ði louerð haet igrete te. þat tou leueſt inne.
74 Bote þou ðo afe i biðbe. ne fcalt tou neuer haue.
Ðe ioie þat iſ in heuene. ne liſ boute care.
Malcuſ þiſ iherðet. iſ fwerðe e gon out ðrawe.
Smot of hire heueð. þat weſ hore lawe.

75 Michael ant gabriel. ant raffael here fere.
Cherubin ant ferafin. a þoufenþ þer were.
Mit tapref ant mit fenferf. to heuene he ir bere.
To hore louerþef bliffe. ho waf ym lef ant bere.
76 Theoboſiuf þe clerc. he wrot hire vie.
Hire nource þat hir wift. i þe toun of afie.
Ho ir þider beren. miþ goþe memorie.
Ant makeþen an chirche. ant þerine maþen hire to lie.
77 Alle þat feke weren. ant þider wolþe go.
Hore hele haueþen. are ahe[le]þen ir fro
Þe heie king of heuene. lef uf to þon fo.
Þat we habben þe bliffe. þat left ouer ant oo.
78 Of þe fwete meiþan. þif if hire vie.
Ð twenteuþe þai if hire. i þe time of iulie.
Ihū chrift þat waf born. of feinte Marie.
Far feinte Maregrete loue. of uf haue mercie.
      Amen. Amen. checun þie Amen.

VARIOUS READINGS AND NOTES

TO

S. MARHERETE.

Fol. 37. a. 11. Pronounce passiun in three syllables. 12. orode. B. 16. icudde. B. better. 21. þene. B.
Fol. 37. b. 2. leaf is plural as well as singular in Saxon English; that it is to be taken here as plural appears by the Saxon copy in Narratiunculæ, by the Latin, and by the easier sense. 14. Margarete. B. 17. pinfule. B. better. 20. lusten. B.
Fol. 38. a. 4. munnid. R. but read munnið, munnieð. B. Margarete. B. and so on. 10. wordliche. R. 11. ha warð as þeo. R.
Fol. 38. b. 1. muchel. B. drehheden B. in margin, drohen in text. 6. Margarete as ha wes ant wiste up oþe feld hire fost'modres schep. þe schimede ant schan. B. This reading must be accepted. 7. wastun. R. his hird hetterliche. B. to be accepted. 8. neomem. R.
Fol. 39. a. 1. while. B. 3. imene. B. ibodi. B. 5. hire. R. hit. B. which seems necessary. iwurðine. B. 11. onswerie. B. 12. bistewwed. B. 15. ra. B. 17. charden. B. 21. þe gios. B.
Fol. 39. b. 4. þeowe. B. 7. ihc. R. 10. as on. R. on ase on. B., both ons by the corrector. 11. Some might interpret the writing as Nai, but see yenet fol. 37. b. 11, yeue fol. 40. b. 5. 15. wari= pæɲჳ, *malignus*, Beda, p. 580, line 40, an adjective taken substantively. 16. utnume. B., dropping N. 20. hise. B. making the pronoun a declinable adjective. 2. Het hire iþe oðer dei bringen biuoren him. B. rather improving the text.
Fol. 40. a. 2. nebschet. R. 7. me to him seolf. B. 9. wondreðe. wið. R. omitting ne. 11. wei. B. accusative. begunne. B. dropping N. 13. 14. wið his wit. B. 15. bisheð, an error; buheð, MSS. 16. to eke. B. The ancient ɟa becomes se in B. 20. 21. aa. R. a. B., the double letter only expresses a very long vowel, the older spelling was á.
Fol. 40. b. 1. forswelten. B. more correctly. 2. þerefter þine ban schulen beon forbernde. B. a better reading. 3. leue. B. dropping N. 4. min iweddede wife. B. definite construction. 11. hit

ne se sare. B. 14. drede. B. more correctly. 18. Perhaps steortnaket: see Glossary. 22. Perhaps eðie: eaðie. B.
Fol. 41. a. 1. feng on, that is onꝼenᵹ. cleopede to criste. B. 3.
naut. B. omitted in R. 4. ne for wele nowþer. B. adds. mine fan
þe feondes imene. B. *my foes the fiends (of hell) I mean* would be
a better reading. 10. seme. B. the correct reading, conj. 3rd
person. 14. walle. R. 17. þe þe. R. 18. 19. remden of reowðe
ant meanden. B. a better alliteration.
Fol. 41. b. 5. unweoten buten wit. R. B. an inconvenient tauto-
logy. 7. an. R. 10. nulle ich. B. 14. feder, the Saxon English
genitive. walle. R. 20. schalt eauer isar ant i sorhe swelten. B.
22. he owraððe warð for. B.
Fol. 42. a. 1. het swiðe bitterliche. B. by combining the readings
the alliteration may be improved. 3. freoliche flesch. B. 4. ant
ant. R. 5. bitrumet. B. Psalm xxi. 14=15. A marginal annota-
tion in a hand of the fifteenth century has interpreted the word
cum ronden. 7. reowfule. B. 10. hunes. R. 11. Psalm xxi.
20=19, oꝼ þam hoꝛnum þaꝛa anhyꝛnna. Paris Psalter. ꝼꝛam hoꝛnum anhyꝛnenðꝛa. Spelmans Psalter. Glede me godd wið þi gleo
ant ȝef me hope of heale. B. 12. þurh þurh. R. 13. iculurene
heowe. B. 17. ouercume. B. ɴ dropped. 21. luðere reue of. B.
Fol. 42. b. 1. muche. B. a syllable dropped. 2. þider. B. þe
heardeste iheortet, omitted by R.: the grammar is remarkable.
3. seorfule. B. with termination of the definite construction. 9.
limel, see Glossary to Layamon. 11. The construction here is
that kind of apposition which the old grammarians called σχῆμα
καθ' ὅλον καὶ μέρος, " sinews " being part of " thee." 12. þu. R.
omits. 15. do is conjunctive in an indirect question. 16. þe
þulli. B. 19. of þe. B. 20. þu schalt. B. 22. selhen. R.
Fol. 43. a. 2. eche wunnen. B. 8. as me reat hire inwart. B.
12. eorliche. R. heorðliche. B. 14. weddede. B. a genitive plural
on an older model than R.
Fol. 43. b. 3. deme. B. ɴ dropped. 9. ne wraðþe þu þe mi wunne
for sahe ᵹ ich segge. B. 12. from þe wit unwitlese. R., from unwitlese. B., but the sense requires þe witlese. 14. ort. R. 19. ut.
R. omits. 20. drakes. B. the true reading, but in fol. 46. b. 6. no
variation. 22. blikeden. B. having the two nominatives for its
subject, while blikede. R. has the nearer only.
Fol. 44. a. 2. ehnen steareden steappre. B. 3. brade. B. a better

plural. ihurnde. B. better for the definite construction. 6. sparklinde. R. After nase=neose. B. thus: Of his speatwile muð sperclede fur ut ant of his nease þurles þreste smoðrinde smoke smecche forcuðest. 8. scheate. B. for lahte. 12. ʒeapede. B. *gaped.* 13. crenge wið. B. 14. forswolhe. B. dropping N. 18. unsehene. B. definite construction. 19. ituðet, that is ʒetẏþeð. 21. an. R. for ant.

Fol. 44. b. 3. eisful, that is, eʒeʃʃul. 4. eile, subjunctive of eʒlan, *to ail*: eılı. B. 6. heieð þe. R. 7. þe. B. for ꝥ. þeos flodes. R. 8. þe flihinde fuheles. B. 10. rune wiðuten euch reste. B. 12. ah sturieð aa mare. R. omits. 14. flede. B. dropping N. 19. loke. B. better: the termination -i at this stage of the language belongs to the indicative present first person. 20. oþe. B. 21. þe. B.

Fol. 45. a. 2. cunnes. B., a frequent spelling, not etymologically correct, but making a short vowel, his. R. 3. i' is a mode of writing ich; iwurðe. B. 5. afatien. R. but aʃatıan means *plaudere*, not *set foot on*. 6. beore. B. dropping N. 13. Wle=ploh, ploeʒ, *fimbria*, fringe. Lye. Andreas 2941. ile. B. 18. read rather edie; eadi. B. The dragon was then not a mere δράκων, but a monster as in heraldry: compare *amidships*. 19. meoppan, *to mar*.

Fol. 45. b. 1. muche. B. dropping a syllable. 6. iborene. B. a plural. blostme. B.: but blosm is a more correct spelling than bloʃtma, since the radix is blos=flos as in †flosere, florere, and *m* is participial for mentum. 7. ant. R. omits. of meidenes bosum. B. 10. walle. R. 14. Here is probably some error in the Latin transcript which the English writer used. Vidi ceruicem meam florentem. MS. Harl. 5327. fol. 18. Vidi crucem meam florentem. MS. Harl. 2801. fol. 64. b. There had been some unintelligible contraction in the earlier Latin. The text agrees here with the earlier English. Narratiunculæ, p. 44=fol. 73. a. 30. 15. hu þe feond. B. 16. sturede aweiwart. B. 17. þe þurs. B. 20. oɲʒel=the French orgueil, coming from a Frankish source doubtless. Here we have a fresh proof of the affinity of the English with the Hellenic. In ὀργᾶν, *to swell*, resides the original idea of both the old English Orgel, *pride*, and of Ὀργή, *anger*: the conjecture about an earlier indifferent meaning of Ὀργή as *temper, disposition*, cannot stand against this comparison. Gebolʒen, *bellied out, puffed*, is in like manner frequently used for *angry*. earheliche auellet. B. *miserably*. 21. hɲaca.

Fol. 46. a. 6. adu. R. 9. ich þonki. B. 14. glistide. R. ʒimstan. R. which hurts the alliteration. 15. unseheliche. B.: this neglect of the final *e* of the plural is a step more towards the modern usage: we have it here only as a slip of the scribe; but a significant slip. 16. anuald þe. B. 21. sorhfulest. B. Marherete. B. Fol. 46. b. 2. bidest. B. 5. ant islein. B. improving the alliteration. 9. þu cwenctest ant. B. makedest. R. 13. igrap þat grisliche þing. B. 16. riht fot. B. swire ant fong. B. 21. houene. R. 22. þa þu weorredest me. B. adds.

Fol. 47. a. 2. þeose word. B., the more ancient neuter plural porð. 3. gast. R. omits. gremie. B. dropping N. 5. astenche. B. dropping N. 6. þe of. B. 9. blissen. B. 13. deorewurðe. B. reache. B. dropping N. 16. te. B. by the usual assimilation. heo. R. omits. to hire. R. doubles. 19. to ꝥ. B. 20. of hweat. R. omits. 22. ediest. R.

Fol. 47. b. 1. unwilles. B. better. milde meiden. B. 2. bigon to breoken on sp. B. 3. Wult tu. B. 7. efden. R. ham. B. adds. 9. nuþe. B. 11. rufines þe rehe. B. 13. nart tu wummon oþre wummen ilich. B. 15. þe. B. 17. blescedest ant makedest. B. mihti rode. B. multiplying the alliteration. 19. lokin. B. 20. wiht. B. 22. bute ich hit am. B. the old way of speaking.

Fol. 48. a. 1. ich ga aa b. B. 2. fohli. R. 4. Looking again at the MS. it seems to read eis weis; eanies weis. B. Wise is feminine, but this may be Ways, æniʒeꞃ peʒeꞃ. 5. þe. B. 10. uuel. R. omits. 12. to. R. 20. lates. R. *manners*. 22. leoteð me ne ne letteð. B.

Fol. 48. b. 1. ham. R. omits. 5. seoluen. B. 7. cuðe þe. R. omits. ouercume. B. dropping N. 11. wlustes. R. a slip of the pen. 13. do. B. dropping N. neauer ne beon idel. B. better. hali monne bone for ham wið hare ahne. B. which clears up the sense. 15. benen aʒein hare unwerste þohtes ꝥ ich in ham þudde þenchen. B. 22. bimon. R.

Fol. 49. a. 2. engles murne. B. omitting N. 3. lahhe. B. dropping N. lihte. B. dropping N. 6. þat sunne. B. see art. 39. Sunne is fem. 9. te licunge of þat fleschliche lust. 11. Read so me for so man, or so men. 17. bið. B. 19. sotliche. B. 21. heorten. B. 22. hwil þat ha. B. nis ter. R. A little later than 1200 A.D. it was customary to change þ into t after s.

Fol. 49. b. 1. Add ne beo from B. 2. ne. R. omits. 3. þat. B.

6. leas. R. omits. 7. sperki. B. 10. of hare heorte. B. 12. wite. B. dropping N. 13. hwuch wunder. B. no doubt the true text. 14. gað forð. B. 19. for ah þeo R. has ant. 22. me sumdel ideruet. B.

Fol. 50. a. 5. wepnen wumme allunge aren. B. enlarging the alliteration. 6. þer. R. þurh. B. 8. alre wundest. R. 10. heo of beoð ierdet. R. 12. wew. R. with a point under the third letter. wei. B. 14. Stew þe. B.: rightly, the verb is active. 16. heane ȝe hali men. B. correctly. 17. Liðebiȝe is a compound of Lithe, *limp, supple*, and Bow, *bend*; it occurs in the Homilies, vol. ii. p. 242. leoðebei. R. 20. wuneð wummon in þe ant hu he com in to þe. B. makie. B. dropping N.

Fol. 50. b. 1. of þin. B. 4. ant hwuch se. B. adds. 5. forȝelde. B. dropping N. 7. Se qð he ich mot nede. B. adds. *So quoth he I needs must.* 9. schulde. B. wið talen. B. 10. iameines. B. 11. ant for. B. omits ant. 12. secho. B. dropping N. 14. al þet measte deal. B. yet bæl is masculine. 15. eadi. B. read in text edie: hure. R. 17. mahe. B. dropping N. riht. R. doubles. 19. mihte of. R. omits. iborhen. B. a better reading from beoρȝen. 21. pite. B. dropping N. R. omits it. 22. ȝef þu wite wult hwi we weoɾið meast rihtwise þeines R. omits.

Fol. 51. a. 1. beoð. B. 3. holes. B. which would be scarcely to be unravelled. 7. ne beo glede. B. dropping N. R. omits. 10. ogodes half. B. 12. uorð warpe. B. dropping N. The Miltonian picture of the alternation of heat and cold in the pit of hell is found as early as Cædmon. Ah þu. B. better. 17. þoa. R. In þe world. R. omits þe. 18. alre þinge. B. 19. na. B. omits. feond. B.

Fol. 51. b. 4. reue. R. 5. beide. B. 6. ich bidde. B. wurðgi. B. 7. ibore. B. dropping N. 9. þat tu þe. B. þe. R. omits. 11. heouenliche. B. 12. ihu crist. B. adds. wurchest. B. 17. Both in B. and R. steortnaket apparently. 21. snercte. B.

Fol. 52. a. 3. to bidden. B. adds. dauiðes. B. 4. fur. R. omits. 5. te lei. R. omits. imine. B. mu. R. 9. deide. R. mi deað. B. 10. þe. R. 13. sunderliche. B. 16. B. differs. 19. druncnin. R. 20. hehte. R. cleope. R.

Fol. 52. b. 4. þe. B. 5. festne mi. R. 9. ant on his deorewurðe sunes. R. omits. 11. ant to cwauien. B. adds. 15. This is apparently loftsong, and so it was read by Sir Frederic Madden, Layamon, vol. iii. p. 439, but it occurs plainly as Lostsong in Si sciret,

NOTES TO S. MARHERETE. 49

fol. 8. b. 14, foL 9. b. 14. with Titus collated. 17. Psalm xciii.= xcii. 19. am. R. 20. þe. B.

Fol. 53. a. 1. bruken in blisse buten ende crunene brihtest. B. 3. weren. R. omits. 5. caplimet is an error arising out of Decapolim et. 6. aheue. B. dropping N. 7. martyrs. B. 8. ward. R. omits. 9. wodschipe. B. wiðblikinde ant bitel brond. B. adds. 11. þe. B. 13. wiðute. B. dropping N. and coming nearer to our modern Without. 14. þat. B. 15. is. R. omits. 16. seolð. R. is. R. We see sometimes tokens of a loss of H in His, as H has been lost in Hit. 19. bide. B. the true spelling. 21. forte cneolin. B. This is now called vulgar English.

Fol. 53. b. 1. domes. B. 6. merkedest þe heouene ant mote wið þi strahte hond ant wið þe icluhte þe eorðe. B. storest. R. Steopan is *rule* generally; as in Introduction to the laws of Edward and Guðrum. For the sense cf. Psalm lxxxix. 7. wiht þe. B. 9. mi. B. 13. liðeliche. R. 17. ham. R. pin. R. 18. ant mi pine. B. adds. hendliche. B. 21. deofle. B. 22. lu ends the folio in R. and begins the next.

Fol. 54. a. 1. him. B. ham. R. This is a plural and a construction κατὰ τὸ σημαινόμενον, after the sense, somewhat as the Hellenes took the same liberty with ὅστις; Δίκη γὰρ οὐκ ἔνεστιν ὀφθαλμοῖς βροτῶν, ὅστις. So above fol. 53. b. 17. 5. þer. B. ahpan in older English. 11. τιþιαιι in O. E. 15. oder. R. 17. ne ne. B., that is *nor ne.* 22. resteð. R. turne. B. dropping N.

Fol. 54. b. 1. for ich kepe þe. B. adds. 2. The modern English Hie representing an old Hian for Hihan, Higan. 4. wealde. B. dropping N. 4. þat ich iwald ah. B. with better rhythm. 6. schulden. R. 9. hwer. R. 12. bluðeliche. 14. icore. B. dropping N. 15. Wealdent of alle iwrahte þinges. 18. al. R. omits. 20. baðe. B. 21. þreo ant tah an in hades to tweamet.

Fol. 55. a. 7. nedunge. B., but adverbs in -lunge, as blindlunge, also existed in the language, as well as those in -unge. 14. þene. B. mit tet ilke. B. inserts merci ant milce. B. 17. of leome. B.

Fol. 55. b. 3. Sihen in the sense *ascend* deserves remark, it is usually *descend.* 4. sweteste. B. 5. dn̄s. dā. sabaot. B. *Lord God of Sabaoþ.* heouenliche weordes. B., that is, peþoð with the new plural termination. 9. Both texts have traces of a defective Latin copy : the true sense was, Et uenientes demones ad reliquias beatæ Margaretæ torquebantur. Infirmi uenientes sanabantur a lan-

H

guoribus suis et credebant. MS. Harl. 5327. fol. 33. b.   12. into antioches burh. B.   13. rgaue. R. gandame. R.   14. inclytæ matronæ. MS. Harl. 5327. fol. 34. a.   Sindentiæ matronæ. MS. Harl. 2801. fol. 65. b.   17. ant hire bonen þat ha bed ;' wrat o boc felle. B.   18. al. R. omits.

Fol. 56. a.   7. ei. R.; this form is also frequent in Layamon and cotemporary authors.   10. fulet. B. *fouled*. ant we bituhe. B.; here N is dropped.   11. iseo. B. dropping N.   14. eorliche. R. eorð. B.

S. MARGARETE þAT HOLI MAIDE.

Line 38. MS. has, For oure louerdes to deþe to beo ibroʒt.
— 146. a fille, so Thomas Beket 946. *filum, thread*.
— 157. swye, probably *silent*.
— 158. whar for *whether*; the pronoun Whether suffers in Islandic the same contraction.
— 289. So MS.
— 317. So MS.

MEIDAN MAREGRETE.

Quatrain 1, line 1. preit. Hickes.
——— 10, — 3. cumraden. H.
——— 17, — 1. *to the ninth generation*.
——— 18, — 2. at all. H. *at a haw, a small berry*. C.
——— 18, — 4. leueð. H. read leuet.
——— 20, — 1. cumnen. H. read cumen.
——— 25, — 1. struen. H.
——— 25, — 2. struen. H. read striuen.
——— 25, — 4. med. H. read mod.
——— 28, — 1. M. speaks.
——— 32, — 1. M. speaks.
——— 33. — 3. insert is.
——— 36, — 1. þe. H. twice.
——— 38, — 1. M. speaks.
——— 39, — 1. read heitte. See 55, 2.
——— 41, — 3. fou. H. absurdly.
——— 45, — 3. mitten by nunnation? Layamon 1194.
——— 47, — 2. hin=hine, H. expressly: he read as printed.
——— 57, — 1. M. speaks.
——— 66, — 3. H. amends todai.
——— 67, — 1. acue. H.
——— 72, — 2. soune. H.
——— 74, — 3. iherdes. H.

SEINTE MARHARETE MODERNIZED.

N.B. Where the modernization differs from the printed text, it is based upon the collation of MS. B. seen in the notes.

Saint Margaret the Maiden and Martyr.

In the Fathers and in the Sons and in the Holy Ghosts name, here beginneth the lifeleading and the passion of Saint Margaret.

After our Lords pain | and his passion, | and his death on rood, | and his arising from death, | and after his upstying (*ascending,*) | as he sty (*ascended*) to heaven, | were many martyrs, | weapon-men both and wife-men, (*men and women*) | to deaths various y-done | for the name of Drihten (*the Lord*) ; | and as y-known champions, | overcame and down-cast | their foes of three kinds, | the fiend and this wicked world | and their leik-hams (*bodies*) lusts ; | and went from these wearinesses | to well-doing and to eternal win(somenesses) | y-crowned to Christ.

Then yet were many more, | than now be, misbelieving men, | who heyed (*extolled*) and herried (*glorified*) | heathen mammets | of stocks and of stones, | works ywrought. | But I a Gods thew (*servant*) | Theotimus y-named | y-learned in Gods law | have y-read and araught (*considered*) | many various leaves ; | and never in no stead | ne might I understand | of none that were worthy | for to be y-worshipt | as, it behoves us, Drihten, | but the high Healer alone, | that is in heaven, | who dwelt, while his will was, | among worldly men, | and cured blind, | the dumb and the deaf, | and the dead raised | to life and to light, | and crowned his y-chosen, | who death drie (*endure*) for him | or any harm : | and all christian men | that be of Christ ycleped | as, if so be, they profit of their name, | have gained the life, | that eternally y-lasteth ; | each baptized in font | in the almighty Fathers name | and in the wise Sons name | and in the Holy Ghosts. | Was in the same time | living in land | the blessed maiden, | Margaret by name, | that fought with the fiend | and with her earthly limbs ; | and overcame and down-cast them: | and I obtained it y-written | of the writer then | all her passion | and her painful death | that she dro (*suffered*) for Drihten. | Let-hearken all who may | and hearing have, | widows and the wedded, | and maidens namely, | let-listen very yearningly, | how they shall love | the loving lord, | and live in maidenhood, | that to him is of virtues liefest, | so that they may | [fol. 38. a.] through the blessed maiden, | that we mention to day, | with maidenhoods mensk (*grace*) | that merry maidens song | sing with this maiden | and with the heavenly herd (*host*) | eternally in heaven.

This maiden whom we mention, | was Margaret y-haten (*called*), | and her fleshly father | Theodosius hatte (*was called,*) | of the heathen folk | patriarch and prince. | And she, as the dearworthy | Drihten (*Lord*) it decreed, | was y-brought into a borough, | to feed and to foster, | from the mickle Antioch | fifteen miles. | Then she had of eld (*age*) | fifteen years ; | and her mother was y-went (*gone*) the way | which worldly men | alone should ywend. | She became to them that had y-wist (*known*) | and y-weened (*thought of*) her | the longer the liefer ; | and all her loved, that on her looked, | as her that loved God, | the heavenly lord ; | and (she) had grace | of the Holy Ghost, | so that she chose him | to love and to lemman ; | and be-took into his hand | the mensk (*grace*) of her maidenhood, | to wit (*look after*) and to wield, | with all herself. | Thus she was and wist (*looked after*), | meekest one maiden, | with other maidens, on the field, | her foster-mothers ownings. | She y-heard on each half (*side*) of her, | how man drew to death | Christs y-chosen | for right belief ; | and (she) yearned and would yearnly (*desirously willed*), | if Gods will were (so), | that she might be | one of the mothers-bairns [fol. 38. b.] that so much dro (*suffered, pl.*) for Drihten. | It be-tid about a stound (*hour, time*) | that there came out of Asia | toward Antioch | of the fiend a foster (one) | to herry (*glorify*) in the high borough | his heathen gods, | Olibrius (he) hatte (*was called*) sherriff of that land, | who all them who believed | on the living God | for-did (*destroyed*) and for-deemed. | But as he went one day his way | he saw this seely maiden, | Margaret, | (as she was and wist, | up on the field, | her foster-mothers sheep, | who shimmered) and shone | all of wult (*aspect*) and westm (*growth*) ; | and het (*ordered*) his hetterly (*persecuting*) herd | to nab her quick. | O. "If she is free woman | I her will have | and to wife hold. | If she thewe (*servant, f.*) is | I choose her to chevese (*concubine*), | and her will free | with gersom (*treasure*) and with gold. | And well to her shall worth (*become*) | for her lovesome leer (*complexion*) | with all that

I wield." | As these knights would warp (*cast*) hands on her, | she began to clepe | and call thus to Christ.

M. " Have, Lord, milce (*mildness*) and mercy of thy woman : | nor let not thou never | my soul be for-lost | with the forlorn, | nor with the lither my life | that be all bloody | be-bloodied with sin. | Jesu Christ, Gods son | be thou ever my glee and my gladdening. | Thee may I aye more hey (*extol*), and herry (*glorify*). | Hold, High Healer, my heart, I beseech thee | in true belief | and be-wit (*look after, protect*) thou my body | which is (to thee) all betaken | from fleshly filths ; | that never my soul | ne be with sin y-soiled | through the leik-hams (*bodys*) lust | which [fol. 39. a.] a little while liketh (*pleases*). | Lord, list now to me, | I have a dear gemstone | and I have it y-given thee | my maidenhood I mean ; | blossom brightest in body | which it beareth ; and be-wit (*look to it*) well | nor let thou never the unwight (*evil wight*) | warp (*cast*) it in the mire, | for it is so lief to thee, | (as) it is to him of things loathsomest. | He warreth and warpeth (*turneth*) | ever there-toward with all kinds wrenches | (*tricks of all kinds*). | Lord, do thou ward me | and wit (*look after, keep*) it ever to thee : | nor thole (*bear, suffer*) thou ever the unwight (*evil wight*) | that he worry my wit, | nor make-to-wane my wisdom : | but send me thy sonde (*thing sent, message*) | High Healer of heaven, | which may couth (*make to know*) me and ken (*make to know*) | how I shall answer | this hateful sherriff. | For I y-see me, Lord, be-stead and be-stood | as lamb with wood (*mad*) wolves, | and as the fowl which is fangen (*taken*) | in the fowlers gryne (*trap*), | and as fish hung on hook, | as the roe y-nabbed in the net. | High Healer (*Saviour*), help me now, | nor leave me never in lither (*bad*) mens hands."

The knights for that she spake thus | turned each again, and say to their lord, | " Ne may thy might have | no communion with this maiden | for ne herrieth (*glorifieth*) she none | of our heathen gods, | but be-lieveth on the Lord, | that Jews for-doomed (*wrongly doomed*) | and heathen on-hung | and heaved up on rood." | Olibrius the lither (*bad*), [fol. 39. b.] when he this y-heard, | changed his cheer, | and bade bring her before him belive (*instantly*). | Soon as she y-come was | he cleped to her thus, | "Couth (*make to know*) me," quoth he, | " if thou art foster of free man, | or a thewe (*servant, fem.*) woman." | The blessed maiden Margaret | soon him answered ; | " Free woman I am and yet Gods thewe." "Yea," quoth he, "and what god | heyest (*extollest*) thou and hear-som-est (*obeyest*)." | "I hey," quoth she, "God the Father, | and his dear-worthy son | Jesu Christ (he) hatte (*is called*), | and to him I have (as) maiden | my maidenhood granted, | and love (him) as lemman | and believe on as lord." | "Yea," quoth he, loud, | "believest thou and lovest him, | who ruthfully died | and drearily on rood?" | "Yea," quoth she, "but they, | who weened for to for-do (*destroy*) him, | thine forefathers, | are for-faren (*gone to ruin*) ruefully | and forlorn litherly (*badly*) ; | and he liveth king-bairn | y-crowned in his kingdom | kaisar of kings | eternally in heaven." | The malignant (one) at these words | became nabbed (*taken*) wrath | and bid her cast into quartern (*prison*) | and into qualm-house (*torment-house*), | till that he had better | bethought him in what wise | he would mar her maidenhood : | and (he) fared him since (*subsequently*) into Antioch, | and heyed (*extolled*) his heathen gods, | as it belonged and lay to | his lither (*bad*) belief. | (He) bade bring her before him, | and she was soon y-brought forth, | and he began to say, | "Maiden [fol. 40. a.] have mercy | and milce (*mildness, compassion*) of thy self. | Take yeme (*care*) of thy youth | and of thy seemly shape and of thy sheen nebship (*face*). | Work after my will | and worship my mammets, | and to thee shall well become | with all that I in world own | and in (my) wield (*power*) have." | Margaret mildest | and of maidens meekest | answered him and said, | "Wit thou if thou wilt, | for he it wot (*knows*) full well, | who has y-sealed to him | myself and my maidenhood ; | that thou ne mayest in no wise | with weal nor with winsomeness, | with woe nor with wandred (*harm*) | nor with no worldly thing | wend (*turn*) me nor wrench (me) | out of the way, | in which I am begun to go : | and unworthy, that wit thou well, | to me be thy words ; | for him alone I love | and have to my belief, | who wieldeth and wisseth (*makes to know, directs*) through his will | winds and the weathers (*storms*) | and all that beset is | with sea and with sun, | both above and beneath, | all bow to him and bend. | To eke (*increase*) this that he is | so mighty and so mainful, | he is loveliest life | for to look upon, | and sweetest to smell, | nor his sweet savour | nor his almighty might | nor his moilless (*spotless*) lovesome leik (*body*) ne may | never lessen nor a-lie (*lie, abate*), | for he a-lies never | but liveth aye in ar (*honour*), | and all that in him lieth, | lasteth aye (*ever*) more." | "Let," quoth Olibrius, "ne beeth this word nought worth. | But a somewhat wit thou, [fol. 40. b.] | but if thou swike (*cease*) em, | my sword shall for-swelt (*kill*) | and for-swallow thy flesh, | and thereafter thy bones shall be for-burned (*burned to dust*) | on burning gledes. | But if thou wilt believe me | thou shalt be my lemman | and my wife y-wedded, | and wield as lady | all that I in wield (*power*) own | and am lord of." | " I give thee well," (*make my acknowledgements*) quoth she, "of thy behest (*offer*), but have thou it (*keep it to thyself*) and thy love: | for I have a liefer (*dearer one*) whom I will for none, | leave nor lose. | Thou swinkest thee (*toilest*) too swithy (*much*) | and warpest (*castest*), (me is woe for it,) | away thy while (*time*); | for to me is all one | thine olecing (*flattery*) and thine awe. | I will betake | my body to every bitterness | that thou canst be-think of, | be it never so derf (*painful*) | to drie (*suffer*) and to dure, | with that (*provided that*) I may | maidens mede have in heaven. | Drihten (*the Lord*) died for us | the dear-worthy lord, | and ne dread I no death | for to drie (*endure*) for him. | He has his mark on me y-sealed | with his own seal; | nor may us (two) neither life nor death | twin (*divide*) a-two." | "Aye," quoth he, " is it so ? | nab her swithy " (*quick*) quoth he to the quellers (*killers*). "Strip her stark naked, | and hang her on high, | and beat her bare body | with bitter besoms." | The a-waried with-laws (*cursed infidels*) | laid so litherly (*badly*) | on her lovely leik (*body*) | that it broke over all | and lathered of blood. | The blessed maiden a-hove her heart | heaved upward [fol. 41. a.] to the heaven, | and began this prayer: | " Lord, in thee is all that I hope, | hold me now my wit so, | and my will to thee, | that it for-worth (*perish*) not | for wo that man may do me. | Nor leave (*give leave to*) thou never my foes, | these fiends of hell, | have nor hold | their hoker (*malice*) of me; | as they would if they might | a-warp (*cast away*) me. | But so ne shall they me, | nor none other that aright loveth thee. | Heavenly Lord, thy name be y-blessed: | Lord look to me, | and have mercy of me: | soften my sore | and salve me mine wounds | that it may neither seem | nor appear by my semblance | that I derf drie (*endure harm*)."

The quellers (*killers*) laid so | litherly (*badly*) on her leik (*body*) | that the blood burst out; | and streamed adown from her body | as a stream doth from a spring. | Olibrius the lither | reeve without ruth | while man yarded (*girded, beat*) her thus | yammeringly, yeyed (*cried*). | "Stop now and stay | thine unwitty words, | and hearken, maiden, to my rede (*counsel*), | and well to thee shall worth (*become*)." | All that there were weapon-men both and wife-men (*both men and women*) out of ruth, | moaned-for this maiden, | and some of em said, | "Margaret, Margaret, | maiden so much worth | if thou well wouldest, (*should be willing*), | woe is us that we y-see | thy soft lovely leik (*body*) | to-loken (*torn to pieces*) so loathly. | Wellaway! [fol. 41. b.] Woman! | What wult (*aspect, beauty*) thou losest | and for-lettest (*lettest go to ruin*) for thy misbelief. | The reeve is ruefully wrath, | and will, I wis, for-do (*do to ruin*) thee; | but love now and believe him, | and thou shalt, woman, most | winsomeness and weal wield." | "O!" quoth Margaret, "wretches unwitty, | wellaway! what ween ye | if my leik (*body*) is to-loken (*torn to pieces*), | my soul shall rest with the righteous. | Sorrow and leiks (*bodys*) sore | is health of souls. | But believe ye, I rede (*advise*) you, | on the loving God, | mighty and mainful | and full of every good, | who heareth them that to him clepe | and openeth heavens gates. | For you I ne will hear, | nor bend to none of your gods, | that dumb be and deaf, | and blind but (*without*) might, | with mans hand y-maked. | But thou workest," quoth she to Olibrius, "the works of thine father the lither (*bad*) one, | of the fiend of hell. | But, thou heathen hound, | the High Healer (*Saviour*) is my help: | and if he have granted to thee | mine leik (*body*) to luken (*tear*); | he will hateful reeve | a-rid my soul | out of thine hands, | and heave her (*it*) to heaven. | Though thou hang me here, | thou grisly gray one | thou lither (*bad*) lion | loath to God. | Thy might shall un-mickle (*diminish*) | and melt to right nought; | and thou shalt be ever in care, | and in sorrow. I game with God | and am glad without end." | He from wrath fared (*went*) | nigh out [fol. 42. a.] of his y-wits, | and bade very hetterly (*persecutingly*) | hang her on high up, | higher than she ere was, | and with sword sharp | and with awls of iron | her lovely leik (*body*) | to wring and to rend. | And she be-saw (*looked*) up on high | and began to say.

"Hell hounds, Lord, have be-trooped me, | and their rede, (*counsel*) that humbleth me. | They have all be-set me. | But thou, High Healer, be | about me to help (me). | A-rid, rueful God, | my soul of swords edge | and of hounds hand; | for ne have I but her (*it*) only. | Loose me, Lord, out of the lions mouth, | and my meek mildship | from the one-horneds horns (*horns of the unicorn*). | Glad me with thy glee, God, | and hope of heal (*salvation*), | that my prayer may | through-drill (*pierce*) the welkin. | Send me thy sonde (*sending*) | in culvers (*doves*) y-leik (*body, form*), | which may-come me to help ; | that I my maidenhood may wit (*look to, preserve*) | unto thee unwemmed (*unpolluted*) ; | and leave me (*give me leave*) yet (*further*), Lord, | if thy will is, to y-see | that a-waried (*cursed*) wight | that warreth against me. | And make-known thy might on me, | Almighty God, | that I him overcome may ; | so that all maidens ever more through me | the more may trust on thee. | Be thy name y-blessed | of all blee (*hue*) bright-est, | to all worlds world (*ages age, age of ages*) | aye on eke-ness (*eternity*). Amen."

While that Margaret spake thus | man to-lec her (*tore her to pieces*) ; | so that the evil reeve | for the strong running | of the bloody stream, | nor none other that there was, | ne might for mickle horror | look thitherwards ; | but (they) hid their heads | the hardest y-hearted | under their mantles, | for the sorrowful sore | that they on her y-saw. | Yet spake and said Olibrius the lither (*bad*), | "What holds maiden, | that thou ne bowest to me ; | nor ne wilt have milce (*mildness*) | nor mercy of thy self ; | or ne feelest thou thy flesh | all to-loken (*torn to pieces*) and to-limbed (*torn limb from limb*) | through that I ordered. | But bow now and bend to me | ere thou die of derf (*harmful*) death | and of dreary ; | for if thou ne dost not, | thou shalt swelt (*die*) through sword | and be all limb-meal to-loken (*torn to pieces*) ; | and then I shall tell (*count*), | when thou all to-torn art | in each ones sight | who sitteth now and seeth thee, | all thine sinews." | "But hateful hound," quoth she then, " though thou all so do | me shendest (*hurtest*) thou nought. | When my soul be before | Gods sight in heaven, | little is it to me | what man may do by me, | and by my body in earth. | But thee it should shame, | thou shame-less shuck (*devil*), | if thou shame knewest, | that such a moot (*debate*) holdest | with a young maiden, | and spillest all thy while (*time*), | and ne speedest nought. | For if I should-work the will of the flesh, | that thou farest all as thou wilt with, | my soul should sink | all so as thine shall | to sorrow in hell ; | and for that I will well (*am very willing*) | that my flesh for-fare (*go to ruin*) here, | that soft Jesu may-crown my soul | in seeliness of heaven; [fol. 43.] | and after doomsday do (*put*) em both together | to weal and to winsomenesses through-wonning (*ever dwelling, everlasting*)." | He became so wrath that for nigh wood (*mad*) | he would y-worth (*become*). | (He) bade his chosen Nubians | cast her in (the) qualm-house (*torture-house*) and man so did soon; and it was as though it were the seventh hour of the day, | that man drew her thus, | into darkest won (*dwelling*) | and worst to won in (*dwell in*). | And she heaved up her hand | and blessed all her body | with the high rood token. | As man led her inward, | she began to bid (*pray*) | this boon (*prayer*) to our Lord. | "Dear-worthy Drihten (*Lord*) | though thy dooms be dern (*secret*), | all they be doughty. | All heavenly things | and earthly both, | bow to thee and bend. | Thou art hope and help | to all that thee herry (*glorify*). | Thou art foster and father | to helpless children. | Thou art the y-weddeds weal, | and widows warrant, | and maidens meed. | Thou art winsomeness of the world, | Jesu Christ kingsbairn; | God kindled (*begotten*) of God, | as light is of leem (*gleam*). | Look, Lord, to me, | my life, my love, my lemman, | milce (*be mild*) to me, thy maiden. | Mine own fleshly father | did (*put*) and drove me away | his only daughter, | and mine friends are to me, | Lord, for thy love, | foemen and fiends (*enemies*). | But thee I have, High Healer, | both for father and for friend. | Ne for-let (*let go to ruin*) [fol. 43. b.] thou me not, | loving Lord; | behold me and help me; | and leave me (*give me leave*) that I may lay eyes | upon the lither (*bad*) unwight (*wicked wight*) | that warreth against me; | and let me deem against him, | Drihten (*Lord*) of doom. | He humbleth and hateth me, | and I it never ne wist | that he had harm of me. | But such is his kind (*nature*) | and so full is of atter (*venom*) | his ond-ful (*full of malice*) heart, | that he hateth each good; | and each holy thing, | and hallowing (*salutary*) is to him loath. | Thou art, Drihten (*Lord*), doomsman | of quick and of dead. | Deem between us two; | nor become-wrath thou for no saying that I say. | For one thing I beseech ever, | and over all, that thou wit (*look after, preserve*) to me | my maidenhood unmarred; | my soul from sin; | my wit and my wisdom | from the witless wight. | In thee is, my Healer, | all that I will. | Be thou all y-blessed, | ord-frum (*beginning*) and end, | and ord (*origin*) aye in eke-ness (*eternity*). Amen."

Her foster mother was one | that frofred (*comforted*) her, and came to the qualm-house (*torture-house*), | and brought to her for food bread | and burns (*brooks*) drink that she by-lived (*ate and drank*). | She then and many more beheld through an eye-hole | as she bade her beads (*said her prayers*). | And (there) came out of a hurn (*corner*) | hyingly (*hastily*) toward her | an unwight (*wicked wight*) of helle | in a dragons leik (*form*) | so grisly that it agrose (*terrified*) em | with that they saw (it). | That unseely-one glistened | as-if it overgilt were; | his locks and his long beard | blazed [fol. 44. a.] all of gold, | and his grisly teeth | seemed of swart iron, | and his two eyes | steeper (*more burning*) than stars | and than gem-stones; | and broad as basins. | In his y-horned head on either half (*side*) | on his high hoked nose | thrust smothering smoke out | of smack (*taste*) for-cuthest (*most known for bad*); | and from his sputtering mouth | sparkled fire out; | and out went his tongue so long, | that he swung her (*it, tongue is fem.*) all about his swere (*neck*), | and it seemed as though a sharp sword | out-of his mouth went, | that glistened as (a) gleam doth, | and lightened all of ley (le𝓏, *flame*); | and all became that stead | of strong and stark stench (*full*), | and of this shuck (*devil*) shadow | it shimmered and shone all. | He stretched him(self) and stirred toward | this meek maiden, | and yawned with his wide jaw | upon her ungainly; | and began to croak | and to crane out (his) swere (*neck*) | as he that her would for-swallow altogether. | If she a-grisen (*terrified*) was | of that grisly grim-one | ne was it not much wonder. | Her blee (*complexion*) began to bleachen, | for the gryre (*terror*) that gripped her, | and for the ferly (*strange*) affright. | (She) forgot her boon (*prayer*) | that she y-bidden (*prayed*) had | so that she might y-see the unseen unwight, | nor naught ne thought thereon that to her now was | y-granted her boon (*prayer*), | but smote smartly adown | her knees to the earth; | and heaved her hands | on high toward heaven, | and with this boon (*prayer*) to Christ thus cleped.

"Invisible God | of each good full, | whose wrath is so grimly, | that hells inhabitants, | and heavens, and all quick things | quake there against (*in presence of it*); | against this aweful wight | that it ne ail me naught, | help me, my Lord! | Thou wroughtest and wieldest | all worldly things; | they hey (*extol*) thee and herry (*glorify*) in heaven | and all the things that eard (*dwell*) in earth, |

the fishes that in the floods | float (*swim*) with fins, | the fowls that
fly by the air, | and all that y-wrought is, | worketh what thy will
is, | and holdeth thy hests but man only. | The sun rakes (*runs*)
her (*its, sun is fem.*) run (*course*) | without each (*any*) rest. | The
moon and the stars, | they wheel by the welkin, | stop not nor
studge | but stir aye more (*evermore*) | nor nowhither from the
way | that thou hast y-wrought em | ne wrench (*twist*) they
never. | Thou steerest the seastream | that it flood ne may | further than thou markedst. | The winds, the weathers (*storms*), |
the woods, and the waters, | bow to thee and bend. | Fiends have
fear | and angels of thine awe (*awfulness*). | The worms (*creeping
things*) and the wild-deer (*wild beasts*), | that on these wild wealds
won, (*dwell*) | live after the laws | that thou hast for em y-locked
(*concluded*), | loving Lord! | And do thou look to me | and help
me thine handywork ; | for all mine hope is on thee. | Thou harrowedst hell | and overcamest, as champion, | the accursed ghost
(*spirit*), | that fondeth (*trieth*) to for-do (*do to ruin*) me. | But
hear me [fol. 45.] now and help me | for ne have I in my need |
none kinds (*of no kind*) courage but thine only. | Against this
evil wit (*look to, protect*) me, | for I trust all upon thee, | and thy
will I worthy (*reverence*) it | dear-worthy Lord ; | that I through
thy strength may stand against him, | and his mickle over-get
(*pride*) that I may a-fell (*make to fall*). | Lo! he fondeth swithy
(*trieth hard*) me to for-swallow, | and weeneth for to bear me |
into his baleful hole | where he woneth (*dwelleth*) in. | But in the
blissful name | I bless me now." | And (she) drew then endlong
(*along*) her(self) | and athwart over thereafter (*after that*) | the
dear-worthy token, | of the dear rood, | which He rested on ; |
and the dragon rushed to her with that same (*instantly*), | and set
his sorry mouth | and unmeasureably mickle, | on high on her
head, | and reached out his tongue | to the fringe of her heels ; |
and swent (*made to vanish*) her in and for-swallowed | into his
wide womb (*belly*). | But to worship for Christ (*to Christs honour*) | and to him to wrotherheal (*damage*) | the rood-token a-rid
her readily | so that she was with (it) y-weaponed, | and worth
(*became*) his bane soon, | so that his body to-burst (*burst to pieces*)
amid-hips, | and the blessed maiden | wholly unmarred | without
every wem (*pollution*) | went out of his womb (*belly*), | herrying
(*glorifying*) on high | her High Healer in heaven. | As she beheld

looking | upon her right half (*side*), | then saw she where sat | an invisible unwight (*wicked wight*) | (a) mickle deal blacker | than any blueman (*Ethiopian*), | so grisly that ne might it | no man lightly a-reckon (*describe*) | and his two hands | to his gnarled knees | smartly fast y-bound; | and she when she saw this | took to thank thus God, | and to herry her High Healer. | " Brightest blee (*complexion*) of all | that ever were y-born | blossom and y-blowen | of maidens body, | Jesu, God and Gods bairn, | y-blessed be thou ever. | I am gameful and glad, Lord, | of thy goodness ; | Kaiser of kings, | Drihten undeadly (*immortal Lord*). | Thou holdest and heavest up true belief. | Thou art well of wisdom | and each winsomeness wakeneth | and waxeth of thee. | Thou art angels weal, | and wieldest and witest (*lookest after, preservest*) em | without woning (*dwelling, ceasing*). | But they game and are glad | all of ghostly mirth ; | But, mighty God, moilless (*spotless*), is that any wonder ? | as yet see I my belief blowing (*blossoming*) ; | and I have y-seen the fiend who weened to for-do me, | he fell even in two ; | and I felt how his foul stench | streamed and stretched against me. | I have y-seen the giant of hell, | hells wolf here a-warpt (*cast away*), | and the manslayer y-slain, | the strong giant y-storven (*dead*). | I have y-seen his overget (*pride*), | and his awful orgueil | ferly (*strangely*) a-felled. | I have y-seen the rood | which a-rid me so readily | of his rueful hreak (*throat*), | how she (*it, rood is fem.*) the baleful worm (*creeping thing*) | and the bitter beast | made to burst. | [fol. 46.] I have y-seen holy | and healing oil, | as it lighted (*descended*) to me, | and I myself smell | of the sweet Jesu, | sweeter than ever any thing | that is on earth. | I have y-seen bliss | and I bless me thereof. | In weal and in win(someness) | (it) is mine that I won (*dwell*) ; | and ne was to me never so woe, | as to me is now well. | Thee (for) it I thank, | tolerant Lord. | I have down the dragon in dust | and his keenship a-cast ; | and he swelteth (*dieth*) | that weened me to forswallow ; | and I am champion and he is craven | that me weened to overcome. | But thee I thank thereof, | that art of kings king | eternally y-crowned, | (the) sorrowful and sorry | and sinful to turn. | The woeful and wretches | and unhappy wissing (*making to know, directing*), | castle of strength | against the strong unwight (*evil wight*), | maidens mirth | and martyrs crown ; | honey-suckle sweetest | and golden yard, | of all golds purest ; |

glistening gemstone of all visible things, | and invisible both ; | sotest (*see Chaucer*) and sweetest | of all ships (*created things*) shaper. | Majesty threefold, | and onefold notwithstanding | trine in three hoods (*persons*), | and in one highship. | High Holy God, | of each good full, | be thou ever and aye | y-herried (*glorified*) and y-heyed (*extolled*) | without blinning (*ceasing*). Amen." | As she had long thus | y-herried (*glorified*) our Lord | came that grisly gray one | creeping her toward, | and held her by the feet, | and as a sorrowful thing | sorrily said. " Margaret maiden, | enough thou hast y-don to me ; | ne pain thou me no more | with thy blessed biddings (*prayers*) | that thou biddest (*prayest*) so oft | for they bind me so sore withal | and make me so unstrong | that I ne feel with me | of-no-kind strength. | Thou hast grimly y-brought | my brother to ground | and slain the slyest devil of hell, | that I in dragons leik (*body, form*) sent, | thee to for-swallow | and to-mar with his mickle might | the main (*might*) of thy maidenhood, | and to make that thou ne were (*should be*) among mankind | y-mentioned on earth. | Thou quenchedst and a-quelledst him with the holy rood ; | and me thou makest to a-starve (*die*) | with the strength of thy beads (*prayers*) | which be to thee so y-minded. | But leave (*give me leave*) me to-go, lady, | last-less (*burden-less*) I thee bid (*pray*)."

This mild maiden Margarete | y-gripped him, that ne agras (*terrified*) her no whit | and hot-fast (*smarting tight*) took him | by the hateful top (*head*), | and heaved him up and dashed him | adown right to the earth ; | and set her foot upon his rough neck | and feng on (*took on*) thus to speak. | "Stop now poor stern-one | and swic (*cease*) now immediately | swicol (*deceitful*) swart devil ; | that thou ne derf (*harm*) me no more ; | for my maidenhood | ne helpeth thee nought. | For I have to (a) help | mine High Healer in heaven ; | and the worlds wielder is aywhere (*each where*), my warrant. | Though thou strong were (*shouldest be*), | he was mickle [fol. 47.] stronger me to wit (*look after, protect*) against this." | Then thumped she upon the thurs (*giant-monster*) | fast with her foot ; | with each one of these words, | "Stop now, evil ghost, | to grumpy me more ; | stop now, thou old manslayer, | that thou ne slay henceforth | Christs y-chosen. | Stop now loathful wight | to a-stink me with the stench, | that from thy mouth styeth (*ascends*). | I am my lords lamb, | and he is my herdsman ; | and I am his thrall | and his thewe (*servant, fem.*) to do all | that his dear will is. | Be he aye (*ever*) y-blessed | who blithe hath y-made me | in endless bliss. Amen." |

While that she spoke thus | of that spiteful wight, | so there lightning came into the qualm-house (*torture-house*) | a leem (*light*) from heaven, | and (it) seemed as though she saw | in the glistening gleam | the dear rood, | a-reach to the heaven, | and (there) sat a culver (*dove*) thereon, | and thus to her cleped. " Maiden blessed one art thou, | Margaret ; | for paradises gates are | yore (*already*) y-opened to-thee now." | And she louted low to her lief lord, | and thanked him yernely (*desirously*), | with inward heart, (did) this maiden ; | and the light a-lay | by little and little | and she be-turned her(self) then | and quoth to the unwight (*evil wight*). | " Ken me " (*make me to know*), quoth she, "quickly | forcuthest (*ill-knownest*) of all things | of what kind (*nature*) thou be." | " Lady," quoth he, " loose thy foot off my neck, | and so lanhure (*immediately*) lithe me (*be gentle to me*), | maiden one blessedest | that I easily may (do so) | and I must needs ; | and nevertheless mine unwill it is, | to do all that thy will is." | The maiden did so, (she) loosed | and lithed (*gentled*) a little | her heel and he began | thus sputteringly to speak. | " Wilt thou wit (*know*) lovesome lady how I het (*am called*) ? | But whatsoever it be about my name, | I have, after Belzebub, | most mens bane y-been ; | and (have) for-swallowed their swink (*labour*) | and to a-swind (*vanish*) y-made (it). | The meeds (*remunerations*) that they (for) many (a) year had y-made, | these with some of my wiles, | I wrenched (from) them adown when they least weened (it) ; | nor never yet ne might me | no man overcome | but thou now that holdest me in bonds | and hast y-blinded me here ; | and art my brothers bane | Ruffinus of hell, | the rehest (*roughest*) and the redewisest (*wisest at counsel*) of all them in hell. | Christ woneth (*dwelleth*) in thee, | for that (reason) thou workest with us | all that thy will is. | Nor nought art thou towoman y-like | me thinketh (*to me it seems*) that thou shinest | sheener than the sun ; | and over all thine limbs | that (they) lighten with leem (*gleam*). | The fingers so frely (*ladylike*) to me seem, and so fair, | and so bright blinking (*throwing light*), | with which thou blessest thee, | and makest the mark | of the dear rood, | that reft from-me my brother, | and (with which thou) me with baleful bonds | bitterly bindest, | so that I may not look (up) | so doth that light leem | and lighten it seems to me." | "Thou fikest" (*deceivest*), quoth she, "foul thing, | but ken (*make to know*) me that-which I ask." | "Wumme (*Alas!*) lady," quoth he then, | "Wo is me of my life ; | except I war aye (*ever*) with the righteous, | of the unseely sinful, [fol. 48.] methinketh, I am all secure. | But the good I am busily about | and em I follow closest, | that try to be clean | without mans consorting | and flee fleshes filths ; | if I might anywise make them to fall | and foul emselves. | Many I have y-warpen (*thrown*) | that weened mine wiles | witerly (*certainly*) to a-start (*escape*) ; | and on this wise, | I let (*cause*) some whiles a clean man | won (*dwell*) nigh a clean woman, | so-that I toward em ne warp (*turn*) nor ne war, | but let em be together. | I let em talk and tattle of good | and truely love em (*one another*), | without evil willing | and all unwrest (*unfit*) wills; | so that either of other as of his own be trusty, | and truly to know (each other) | and the securer be | to sit together and game by em one (*themselves alone*). | Then through this security seek I erst (*earliest*) upon em | and shoot swithy (*very*) secretly | and wound ere they wit (*know*) it, | with very venomed unguent | their unwary hearts ; | lightly erst (*earliest*) of all, | with lovely wults (*looks*) | with hot beholding either on other, | and with perilous speech speed them together, | so long that they tussle together and toy. | And then thump I into em loving thoughts | on erst (*earliest*) against their will, | and so waxeth that woe | through (*because*) that to em it seemeth good. | And then and when they let me, | [fol. 48. b.] and they hinder me not | nor ne stir em selves | nor ne stand strongly against (me) | I lead em in the lins (*pools*) and in the loathly letch (*swamp*) | of the sooty sin. | If they will withstand | mine unwrest (*unfit*) wrenches | and mine swicful (*deceitful*) swinges | wrestle they must and withstand emselves | but me down-cast they ne may | er they emselves overcome. | Loath (it) is to me | and natheless by-need I do it ; | ken thee (*make thee know*) how they may | best overcome me. | Loose me and lithe (*gentle*) me | lady the while | and I to-thee will say.

These be the weapons | that me worst wound | and wit (*protect*) em unwemmed (*unpolluted*) | and strengthen em stalwardliest against me, | and against em(selves) and their wicked lusts ; |

that be, to eat meekly and drink meeklier; | do (*put*) the flesh in
some derf (*harm*), | and never ne be idle; | holy mens boons
(*prayers*) for em with their own | and bedeful (*prayerful*) thoughts
that they shall think; | among their prayers | against their un-
suitable thoughts that I thump into em | to think (that) it is through
me | that their lust leadeth em | to work to woe; | to think if they
bow to me | to how bitter (a) beast they bow | and whose love
they lose; | that lovesome thing | maidenhood maidens mensk
(*grace*), and the love | of the lovely lord of heaven | and the love-
some queen, the angels lady, | and humble-ones make em (selves) |
with the heavenly herd (*host*) | and unmensk (*disgrace*) emselves |
among earthly [fol. 49.] men | and for-lose the love | not only on
high in heaven | but of low eke in earth; | and make the angels to
mourn | and us in much mirth, | to laugh so loud, | who see em alight
so low of so very high, | from the highest in heaven | to the lowest
in hell. | This they must often mention by emselves. | (They must)
think how swart (a) thing | and how sooty is sin; | think of hell
woe | of heaven-rykes (*kingdoms*) winsomeness; | and mention often
their own death and Drihtens (*the Lords*), | and the grisliness and
gryre (*terror*) | which be at the doom; | think that the fleshes
lusts | alieth very soon, | the pain for it lasteth aye (*ever*) more; |
and whensoever men fall-guilty a whit | go anon forthright | that
they delay it not | to shew it in shrift, | be it never so little | nor
so light sin. | That is under sun | of things to me (the) loathest |
that (a) man run oft | to shrift of his sins; | for little I may
make | to micklen (*increase*) immensely | if man hides and heles
(*conceals*) it. | But soon as it y-shewed is | be-rue-ingly in shrift, |
then (it) shames me (*I am shamed*) | and therewith (I) flee from em |
shuddering as-if I were y-shent (*hurt*). | Though so forth and so far
(i. e. *with these remedies*) they may step again in | softly to love, |
so-that they nowise ne shall stay their hearts | nor stint nor with-
stand | the strength of my swinges, | while they samned be; | ne
is there bote (*remedy*) none | but to flee thence; | so-that neither
nowhere alone with other [fol. 49. b.] | (they) ne see em (*they see
one another*) | nor samn (*meet*) nor sit together, | without a wit-
ness, | who may see what they do | and hear what they say. | If
they thus let (*hinder*) not | but þave (*permit*) and þole (*endure*) |
and ween though (*nevertheless*) to out-wrench (*twist*) | I lead them
with leasing (*lying*) love | by little and little | into so deep (a)

K

dump (*swamp*) | that they drown therein, | and strike in em sparks | of lusts so lither (*bad*), | that they burn away inwardly with (them) | and through the burning go-blind, | so-that they have no sight, | emselves to be-see (*see to*). | The main (*might*) of em melteth | and for-worth (*becomes ruined*) their wit | and warreth their wisdom | so that ne will they nought wit (*know*), | that that they ought to wit (*know*) well. | Look now (a) wonder. | They be so clean overcome | and so have I blinded em, | that they blindly go | and for-see (*regard not*) God | and emselves (they) forget; | so that they litherly (*badly*) | when they least ween, | ferly (*strangely*) fall, | foully and fennily (*dirtily*) | in fleshly filths. | For a lust that a-lieth (*abates*) | man in a moment loseth | both the love of God | and the worlds worship. | But them (*as to them*)' that stalwart be | and stark (*strong*) against me | so that they against me and my wrenches | watchful em(selves) ward; | so evil me thinketh (*it seems to me*) thereof | that I am all dreary | till that they be through a-dorven (*harmed*), | and (I) am in their beds | so busy em about [fol. 50. a.] | that some wise they shall | em(selves) sleeping soil. | But the rood-mark | marreth me over all | and most at the end." | And with this same (word he) began | to yey (*cry*) and to yure (*chatter*). | "Margaret maiden | to what shall I y-worth (*become*) ? | Mine weapons are wholly warped (*turned*). | Yet were it (*optatively*) through a man | as it is now through a woman. | This yet thinketh me (*seems to me*) worst, | that all thy kin | that thou art y-come of | be in our bonds; | and thou art out-broken em, | of all wonders greatest, | that thou by thee alone (*thyself*) hast | overgone thy father and thy mother, | mays both and mayen (*relatives male and female*), | and all the end (*corner of the land*) that thou and they have y-dwelt | and Christ alone hast y-chosen | to lemman and to lord. | (Thou) beatest us and bindest | and to death for-deemest. | Why! weak be we now | and nought worth by all means | when a maiden our mickle | overget (*pride*) thus felleth." | "Stay," quoth she, "sorry wight, and say to-me | where thou most wonest (*dwellest*), | of what kin art thou y-come | and thy kind ken (*make to know*) me | and through whose hests (*orders*) humble ye | and harm their works." | "But say to-me, seely maiden, | whence is to-thee y-leaved (*permitted*), | in thine lithebending limbs | so stalwart strength; | of what kind (*from what nature*) cometh to-thee | thy love and thine belief, | that layeth me so low. | Cuth (*make to know*) me and ken (*make to know*) me | why the worlds wielder | woneth in thee | and how he came, woman, to thee; | and I will make thee | aware of all my wiles." | " Stay thee, storve (*fierce of face*), | and [fol. 50. b.] and still be thine asking. | Yea, ne art thou not worthy | to hear my voice, | awaried (*cursed*) foul wight, | and much less to understand | so dern (*secret*) (a) thing and so dark | of Gods digelness (*secrecy*) ; | and whatsoever I am | through Gods grace I it do | and am, (of) free-gift undeserved, | that he hath me y-granted, | for to yield it to-himself. | But quickly cuth (*make to know*) me and ken (*make to know*) | what I ask after." |

" Satanas the unseely | that for his pride | from paradise lighted so low, | he is kaiser and king | y-crowned of us all; | and to what purpose should I tell thee | and my tale tell | lovesome lady | of our kind (*nature*) and our kin, | that thou canst thyself y-see, | in Iannes and in Mambres books y-briefed (*abridged*). | Such fear I feel, | for sights that I y-see; | Christ seek to (*visit*) thee, | that speak I ne dare not, | but (am) doleful and dolorous | droopiest of all things. | Though since thou wilt wit | we live in the luft (*air*) | of all the most deal (*mostly*), | blessed maiden | and our ways | be above with the winds, | and (we) be ever watchful | to work all the woe | that we ever may to mankind, | and mostly righteous men | and maidens as thou art. | For Jesu Christ Gods bairn | was of maiden y-born | and through the might of maidenhood | was mankind (*human nature*) y-borowed (*bailed*) | (*through it was*) be-nabbed (*taken*) and bereaved us | all that we owned. | Now thou wittest lady | what thou to wit wouldest, | where we most won (*dwell*), | and why we most humble | and hate the maidens. | Yet if thou wilt wit | why we war most | (the) righteous against | I answer for [fol. 51. a.] ond (*malice*) | that eats ever and aye | our hearts. We wit (*know*) | they be y-wrought | to sty (*ascend*) to the stead | from which we fell | and to us it seemeth odious | and very hateful of that ; | so the teen (*vexation*) tendeth (*fires*) us | that we become wood (*mad*) | with the grimness that agriseth (*vexes*) us | ever against the good. | That is our kind (*nature*) | (that I should tell thee) | and to be sorrowful and sorry | of each mans seeliness (*happiness*) | and game, when he guiltieth (*becomes guilty*) ; | and never more be glad | but for evil only. | This is our kind (*nature*) moilless (*spotless*) maiden. | But dear

Drihtens (*Lords*) lamb | lithe (*gentle*) me a little | and loose, lady, thy foot | that sits-on me so sore | I halse (*entreat*) thee in Gods name | high heavenly father | and on Jesu Christs be-half | his only seld-like (*wondrous*) son. | Man nor woman ne may | never more warp (*cast*) me hence | but (do) thou bright bird (*or bride*) | bind me on earth, | and warp (*cast*) thou me not | nether into hell. | For Solomon the wise | while he here wonned (*dwelt*) | be-tuned (*enclosed*) us in a tun, | and came men of Babylon | and weened for to have | gold hoard y-found | and brake the vat (*vessel*) | and we forth (went) and filled then | the wideness of the world." | " Still be thou, still, | poorest of all, stern-one, | nor shalt thou old shock (*devil*) | moot with ne no more. | But fly sorrowful thing | out of mine eyesight | and dive thither where thou man | may damage no more." | With that same the earth twinned (*parted in two*) | and be-tuned (*inclosed*) him, and he roaring | rode ruglingly (*sprawlingly*) into hell. | On the morrow sent Olibrius [fol. 51. b.] the lither (*bad*) his men | to bring her before him, | and she blessed her(self) | and came boldly forth. | Strak (*strode*) men thitherward then | out of every street | for to see the sorrow | that man would lay | upon her lovely body, | if she to the reeves rede (*advice*) | should neither bend nor bow. | " Maiden," quoth he, " Margaret, | yet I bid thee and bode (*announce*) | that thou work my will | and worship my mammets (*idols*) ; | and the tide and the time | on which thou wert y-boren | shall be y-blessed." | " Nay," quoth she, " care I nought, | that man should bless me so. | But it were thy gain, | that thou who goest unblessed | and thy god both | after blessings should go, | and should hey (*extol*) God Almighty, | high heavenly father | and his seld-couth (*wondrous*) son, | who is sooth (*true*) man | and God none the less. | But thou worshipst witless wights | as thou art worthy, | bloodless and boneless | dumb and deaf. | And yet thou workest worse, | for the unseen unwights (*invisible evil beings*) | won (*dwell*) them within, | and thou as thy lords | lovest em and heyest (*extollest*)." | Him it began to grim-make | and of grumpiness he gret (*cried*), | " Strip-ye her stark naked | and heave her on high up | that she may hang for meed (*as her reward*) | for her hoker (*insolence*), | and tend ye (*kindle*) her body | with burning tapers. | The dribbles undoughty so did soon | so-that the snow white hide | swarthened as it snarkt (*frizzled*), | and burst into blains | so-that arose up all over; | and her [fol. 52. a.] lovely leik (*body*) | crackled with the ley (*flame*); | so that all screamed | that on her soft sides | y-saw that ruth | and she began. Davids boon (*prayer*). | "High Heavenly God | with the healing fire of the Holy Ghost, | mankinds frofer (*comfort*), | fire mine heart, | and let the ley (*flame*) of thy love | lighten my loins." | Yet to her (?) quoth Olibrius of reeves the litherest; | "Believe, maiden, my rede : | work what I will | ere than thou thy life litherly for-let (*quit*)." | "Litherly I should-live," quoth Margaret, "if I thee should-believe. | But if in this day my soul | is dear-worth and dear into eternal life ; | thou swinkest (*labourest*) thee sorely | and ne speedest no whit; | nor mayest thou nor thine unwight | nought work on me | a maiden, alone as I am: | but you weary yourselves. | One lord hath my loves | sunderly y-sealed | and hath for my gemstone that I granted him | y-yarked (*prepared*) und y-given me | (the) champions crown." | Then worth (*became*) the reeve wood (*mad*) | and bade in wood (*mad*) wise | and in great wrath | bring forth a vat | and fill it with water; | and bind her both | the feet and the hands, | and dash her to the bottom (of it), | that she death might drie (*suffer*) | and might drown therein. | Man did (*it was done*) soon as he hat (*ordered*), | and she beheld on high up | and cleped toward heaven. | "King of all kings, | break now my bonds, | that I and all that see it | may hey (*extol*) [fol. 52. b.] thee and herry (*glorify*). | May this water werth (*become*) | to-me winsome and soft, | and leave (*permit*) me that it to me | bath be of bliss | and fulht (*baptism*) of font-stone, | healing and leem (*light*) | of eternal health (*salvation*). | Let-come the holy ghost | in culvers (*doves*) likeness | that in thy blissful name | it-may-bless these waters. | Fasten with fulht (*baptism*) | my soul to thyself; | and with these same waters | wash me within | and warp (*cast*) from me away every sin | and bring me to my bright bower | bridegroom of win(-someness). | I underfong (*undertake*) here fulht (*baptism*) | in dear Drihtens name | and in his dearworth Sons | and in the Holy Ghosts | one God in godhood | y-tunet (*inclosed*) and undoled (*undivided*)." | She ne had but y-said so | when all the earth began to quake | and came a culver (*dove*) | burning bright | as though it burned, | and brought a golden crown and set it | on that seely maidens head. | With that same her bonds | broke and burst; | and she as sheen as shining sun | went up therefrom |

singing a lusty song (*song of pleasure*), | that David the witega (*prophet*) | wrought far before that | for Christ as worship. | "My lovesome lord," quoth she, "he kenneth (*makes known*) as king | that he ruleth aright. | Terror and strength | are his shrouds | and he is on-girt with-em | so-that they comely fare | and seemly sit." | "Come," quoth the culver, | with shilling (*ringing*) steven (*voice*), | "and sty (*ascend*) to the weals (*well being*) | and to the wins (*joys*) in heaven. | Blessed wert thou, maiden, | that thou chose maidenhood | which is queen of all mights [fol. 53. a.], for thou shalt aye without end | brook (*enjoy*) bliss. Amen."

In that ilk time | turned to our lord | five thousand men, | yet without y-told (*counted*) | children and women, | who were all anon right-out in Christs kingly name, | as the reeve hat (*bade*) | of head becarven | in a borough of Armenia | Caplimet y-named; | all herrying God | with up a-heaved steven (*voice*), | and they stie (*ascended*) all as-martyrs | with mirths to heaven. | The reeve reddened all of grumpiness | so (it) him grim-made | and worth (*became*) so wroth and so a-wood (*mad*) | that he in wood (*mad*) wise | doomed her to death | and hat (*bade*) in hot heart | that man her head | with shimmering and sharp sword | should-to-twin (*part in two*) from the body. | (Then) laid hands on her | they that y-haten (*bidden*) were | and bound her so-that the blood | burst out at the nails; | and without the borough | (they) led (her) to behead (her). | "Maiden," quoth Malcus, | "stretch forth thy swere (*neck*) | sharp sword to underfong (*undertake*) | for I must thy bane be, | and that to-me is wo; | for if I might there-against —— | for I y-see God (him)self | with his blessed angels | betroop thee about." | "Abide me, brother, then," quoth she, | "while that I y-bid me (*pray*), | and betake my ghost | and my body both | to ro (*repose*) and to rest." | "I bid (*pray*)," quoth he, "that thou do boldly, | while thee well liketh (*it pleases*)." | And she began on her knees to kneel adown | and blithe with this boon (*prayer*) bore on high | (her) y-heaved up hands toward heaven [fol. 53. b.] | "Drihtin, lewds (*peoples*) lord, | though thine runes (*secrets*) derne (*hidden*) be and dark | they all be doughty (*excellent*). | To me is death here y-doomed now, | and with thee life is lent (me). | Thy mild milce (*mercy*) I thank for-it. | Thou folks father of frumship (*primitiveness, the beginning of things*) | shapedest all that yshapen is. | Thou, wisest wright of all, | markedest (out) earth, | thou steersman (*ruler*) of sea stream, | thou wisser (*making to wit, director*) and wielder | of all wights that y-wrought be | visible and invisible. | Bow thine ears healing (*saving*) God | and bend to my boons (*prayers*), | I bid and beseech thee; | [thou art to me weal and win (*joy*)], | that who soever book writes of my lifelode (*life-leading*), | or gets it (when) y-written, | or holdeth it and hath (it) oftenest in hand | or who soever it readeth | or to the reader blithely listneth, | wielder of heaven, | worth (*let become*) to-em | soon all their sins forgiven. | Whoso in my name | maketh chapel or church | or findeth in em light or lamp, | the leem give em lord | and grant em of heaven. | In the house where woman pineth of child, | so soon as she mentioneth my name, | hyingly (*hastily*) help her, | and y-hear her boon (*prayer*), | so that in the house ne be y-born | none mis-limbed bairn, | neither halt nor humpbacked, | neither dumb nor deaf, | nor y-derved (*vexed*) of devils, | but whosoever my name mentioneth | and hath it oft in mouth [fol. 54. a.], | lovely Lord, at the last doom | release em from death." |

With this then it thought (*seemed*) | as though a thunder dinned, | and came a culver (*dove*), bright | as though she burned, from heaven, | with a rood lightning | of light and of leem (*gleam*), | and the maiden diving (*sinking*) | fell down to the earth; | and came the culver | and a-hran (*touched*) her | and raised her up with the rood. | And said her sweetly to | with sotest (*sweetest*) of all stevens (*voices*); | "Blessed art thou, maiden, | among all women; | (in) the oil healing and holesome, | that thou hast y-sought after, (*that is, the unction of the Holy Spirit*); | and all sinful men | (hast) y-mentioned in thine blessed beads | and in thine boons (*prayers*). | By myself I swear, | and by my heavenly herd (*host*), | that thy beads (*prayers*) be to-thee | truly y-tithed (*granted*), | and for all them y-heard, | for whom thou y-bidden (*prayed*) hast : | and much more is given to them | that thy name mind, | and (there is) granted to them many a thing, | that ne is not now y-mentioned. | And wheresoever thy body | or any of thy bones be, | or book of thy pain, | let-come the sinful man, | and let-him-lay his mouth thereupon, | I salve (*cure by unction*) for him his sins, | and ne shall none unwight (*evil wight*) won (*dwell*) in the wons (*dwellings*), | wherein thy martyrdom is y-written : |

but all of the house shall glad-them in Gods grith (*peace*) | and in
ghostly love ; | and to all that to thee bid (*pray*), | to them I
grant to yark (*prepare*) for them | of their sorrows (*bpoca*) a
remedy. | And thou art blessed | and the stead on which thou
restest, | and all that through thee, | shall turn to me. | [fol. 54. b.]
Come now forth, bride, | to thy bridegroom. | Come now, love, to
thy life, | for I copny (*expect*) thy coming. | Brightest bower
abides thee. | Love, hie to me. | Come now to my kingdom. |
Leave the lewd (*people*) so low, | and thou shalt wield with me |
all that I own, | bride of all brightest." | The steven (*voice*)
stopped, | and she stood up | and began to bid (*pray*) | them,
that her about were | and her death be-wept, | that they should
thole (*endure it*), | and said, " Let-alone and leave your lament |
and your loathly bere (*voice*), | and be glad all with me, | that wish
me good, | for ye have y-heard, | if ye hearkened aright, | what
the High Healer (*Saviour*) | hath me be-hoten (*promised*) ; | and
as ye love yourselves | love-like I lere (*teach*) you, | that ye have
my name | mickle in mind, | for I shall bid (*pray*) for them |
blithely in heaven, | who oft mind my name | and mention (it) on
earth. | With blithe heart bear me company, | for to herry (*glo-
rify*) the king, | who hath y-chosen me. | (The) worlds wright and
wielding all is (he), | whom I thank therefore. | Thee I hey (*extol*)
and herry (*glorify*), | Heavenly Healer (*Saviour*). | For thy dear-
worthy name | I have y-drien (*suffered*) harm, | and nab (*take*)
death now. | And nab (*take*) thou me to thee, O God, | of all that
good is | origin and end. Be thou aye y-blessed, | and thy bliss-
ful son, Jesu Christ | by his name with the Holy Ghost, | that
glides (*proceeds*) of you-two both, | threefold and yet one | in per-
sons totwinned (*divided*), | untodealed (*undivided*) in highship, |
undoled (*undivided*), | y-tied and y-tuned (*inclosed*), | one God in
[fol. 55. a.] main (*might*). | Worship and worthiness | worth (*be-
come, be*) to thee only | from world (*age*) unto world aye in eter-
nity." | After this boon (*prayer*), | then bent she the neck, | and
quoth to the queller, | " Do now, brother, hyingly (*hastily*), | what
to-thee is y-hoten (*ordered*)." | " Nay," quoth he, " ne will I not, |
for I have y-heard how | Drihtens dear mouth | hath with thee
mooted." | " Thou must," quoth the maiden, " of need do it ; |
for if thou dost not, | ne shalt thou have with me | a dole of
heavens realm." | And he with that ilk heaved up | (the) keenest

of all weapons, | and smot smartly adown, | so-that the dint dived in, | and the sharp sword | and also smart | shore her by the shoulders, | and sawed her throughout : | and the body bowed | and bent to the earth. | The ghost anon stie (*ascended*) up | into the starry bower, | blithe to heaven. | He that the dint gave | gret (*cried*) with loud steven (*voice*), | " Drihten, do to-me mercy for this deed, | of this sin, Lord, look (thou) me now salve (*cure by unction*)," | and (he) fell adown for fear | on her right side. | Came flashing then | the angels of heaven | and sat and sang on her body | bilewit (*innocent*) and blessed it. | The fiends that were there, | deadly damaged took to cry, | " Margaret, maiden, lithe (*gentle*) now | lanhure (*immediately*) and loose our bonds. | We be well assured, | that there ne is none lord, | but God on whom thou believest." | There turned then through this | to Christ very many, | and there came [fol. 55. b.] dumb and deaf | to her body as it lay, | and were bettered all. | The angels, as they bore the soul | in their bosoms, sie (*ascended*) to heaven | and sang as they stie (*ascended*) up | with sweetest steven (*voice*), | " Holy is, Holy is, Holy is, the Lord | of heavenly hosts. | Heaven is full and earth | of his worshipful weals (*well being*). | Wielder of all wights, | in highness heal (*save*) us. | Blessed be the bairns coming, | who comes in Drihtens name | Hosannah in the highest." | With that then began | to shout and to yell, | and drew all to her body, | who were infirm | and (they) had their healing. | Came I Theotimus, | and took her lovely leik (*body*) | and bore it into a borough of Antioch | with mirth un-y-measured, | and put it in a grave-stone (*stone coffin*) | in her grandams house | that was y-cleped Clete (*Syncletica*). | I ought well to wit (*know*) this | for in pain of prison | where she was y-put in, | I her flutting (*subsistence*) found, | and fleshly food. | And I saw where she fought | with the fearful fiend ; | and her boon (*prayer*) was that I it | should write on book-fell (*vellum*), | and her lifelode (*lifeleading*) | let (*cause*) all to set (*to be set*) on leaves, | and send it soothly y-written | wide through the world. |

Thus the blessed maiden, | Margaret by name, | in the month that in our language, Old English, is ynamed Afterlith, (or) July in Latin, | on the twentieth day | with tortures died [fol. 56. a.] and went from woes | to eternal wins (*joys*), | to (the) life that aye lasteth | without bale, | to blisses without woe, everlasting. |

L

All ye, who this heartily | have y-heard | in your beads (*prayers*), | the blithelier | mind-ye this maiden, | that she with the ilk (*same*) boon (*prayer*) | that she bad (*prayed*) on earth | may bid (*pray*) yet for you | in the bliss of heaven ; | where she shineth sevenfold | sheener than the sun | in sy (*victory*) and in selth (*felicity*), | more than any mouth | it could mention-of, | which man nor woman | ne may, who is of flesh y-soiled, | O ! that we among the angels | through her earnings (*merits*) may yet y-see her | and y-hear her sing. Amen. | Great glory to God the ther | and his Son y·samod (*along with him*) | to the Holy Ghost y-heyed (*extolled*), | to these three in one | y-thaned (*attended*) of angels | and of earthly men | aye without end. Amen.

ON THE LANGUAGE OF ST. MARHERETE.

1. Having before us specimens of our language at different times, we shall do well to turn our attention to some of its changes.

2. From the earliest footing of our race in this country the spoken language has been called English. When Beda speaking of a bishop of Rochester says he was skilled Saxonica lingua (p. 190. 9), his translator gives it "in Englisc" (p. 622, line 2). Ælfric in the preface to his translation of parts of the Pentateuch tells us he translates from Latin into English. Se þe awent of Ledene on Englisc. æfre he sceal gefadian hit swa þ þ Englisc hæbbe his agene wisan. (Thwaites, p. 4.) At the end also of his homilies he declares he will turn no more of them into "English." Ic cweðe nu þæt ic næfre heonon forð ne awende godspel trahtas of Ledene on Englisc. (Homil. vol. ii. p. 594.) In the foreword to the second book of Homilies, Ic Ælfric munuc awende þas bóc of Ledenum bócum to Engliscum gereorde. þam mannum te rædenne þe þæt Leden ne cunnon. *I Ælfric, monk, turned this book from Latin books to (the) English language, for the men to read who ken not the Latin.* In the letter to Sigwerd, Ðu bæde me for oft engliscra gewritena. (De veteri testamento. Lisle. sign. A.) *Thou*

bade me oft for English writings. In Sigwulfs translation of Alcuins questions þæt is on englisc. (62. P. 22. ed. B.) And never otherwise till these latter days, when men had unlearned their native tongue. The poem we have now printed dates the martyrdom of Saint Margaret in July in the month called in "Old English" Efterliðf. (fol. 55. b. 20.) Among ˏthe Saxons June was Se ærra liða and July Se æftera liða (Hickes, vol. iii. p. 107) ; our author therefore calls the tongue of his forefathers Old English. In the Liflade of St. Juliana, "of Latin iturned into English," he calls his own speech English. (fol. 56. a. 20.) It is now the custom to talk of Anglo-Saxon, and the term Semi-Saxon has been invented, out of a love of technicality for English between the dates 1100 and 1230. (Preface to Layamon, p. vii.)

3. Not only, however, was the ancient language English, but as naturally would follow, the whole race of people, whether Angles, Saxons, Jutes or Frisians, were, when spoken of as one, Angelcynn, English-kin; and the whole country, wherein they dwelt, from the Grampians to Dover was called England. While on the mainland the name of the Saxons prevailed it gave way in this island to that of the Angles. On this point we can only trust our own folk, for writers abroad would readily substitute the continental appellation for that by which the islanders spoke of themselves. It has, however, been "inferred from the many differences in dialect" collected by Mr. Garnett that "the literature of the Angles to be currently understood, required translation into the Saxon idiom." Mr. Garnett collected chiefly differences in the use of vowels, which have never in the native utterance of our speech been carefully discriminated. There is no difficulty whatever in reading all existing records, talk as they may about dialects, from all parts of the kingdom as one language, and these vowel differences are no more than what exist between Will, Would, between Velle, Volui, nor can they embarrass a hearer more than for a moment. Most, if not all, of the essays on English dialects go upon several assumptions, which in many cases appear to be quite unfounded. Thus in the paper by Mr. Garnett there is a total absence of evidence that the writers of the glosses in the Psalter (MS. Cott. Vesp. A. i.) and Lindisfarne Gospels (MS. Cott. Nero, D. 4.) were Northumbrians at all; and as to the Ritual, the writer directly connects himself with Ockley in Wessex, near Guildford.

Mr. Garnett in another place (vol. ii. p. 78), rather against his own tale, says, "with the exception of one or two isolated words, there is nothing that can be satisfactorily referred to that class of dialects (Northumbrian) either in the Durham texts or the Rushworth Gospels."

4. Well, if we appeal to our own people, we find them speaking of the whole Teutonic race settled here as Angles. In his edition of the Chronicle (Nom. Loc. Expl. p. 27. a.) Gibson tells us that Egbert by promulgation of an edict "Englaland vocari terram hanc jussit," but Gibson was misled by a document now known to be forged. Beda, who died long before this supposed edict, dates from the "adventus Anglorum in Britanniam" (H. E. p. 59, line 12), "ex quo Britanniam petierunt Angli" (H. E. p. 143, line 11), and his expression is accepted by the native translator " Syþþan Angelcynne Breotone gesohte" (p. 565, 29). Beda tells also of the spread of chanting from Kent over all England, " Sed et sonos cantandi in Ecclesia, quos eatenus in Cantia tantum noverant, ab hoc tempore per omnes Anglorum ecclesias discere cœperunt" (p. 143, line 16), and the translator in like manner gives us " through all churches of Angelkin " (p. 565, 35). Beda calls the archbishop of Canterbury archbishop of the "English" church (p. 141, line 17), while at the same time, when he comes to distinctions of tribes, he settles Kent with Iutes (p. 52, line 35). When he has to mention the races which peopled these islands he says nothing of the Saxons, but flings all the Gothic tribes together as English. "Denique omnes nationes, et provincias Britanniæ, quæ in quattuor linguas, id est, Britonum, Pictorum, Scottorum et Anglorum divisæ sunt, in ditione accepit." (p. 109. 7.) Forðon eall Breoton cynn and mægðe ða syndon in feower gereorda todæled. Þ is Brytta and Peohta and Scotta and Angla. in anweald onfeng. (p. 528. 7.) In Alfreds laws (p. 27), On Æþelbryhtes [dæge] þe ærest fulluht onfeng on Angelcynne=Qui primus in Anglorum gente babtizatus est. (p. 492.) Ine, king of the West Saxons, generalizes his laws by the term Englishman, not Saxon. (xxiv.) These citations might be continued. It is however plain enough, that with Beda, the only ancient authority on whom we can place much reliance, the very tradition of our own lips coincides, for we call the country England because it was inhabited by the English.

5. The phrases used by writers at a distance commonly spring from their own view of events, as bearing on themselves; thus Vitalianus addresses Oswy, king of Northumberland, as "Rex Saxonum" (Beda, p. 138, line 27), while it is certain that Northumberland was not said to be inhabited by Saxons at all.

6. England, Angles and English are therefore the true names of our land, our fathers, and our native speech. The term Anglosaxon is of modern invention; the catalogue of the manuscripts in Glastonbury Abbey drawn up in 1248 describes the old Homilies as "Sermones Anglici, vetusti, inutiles," a Saxon book of medicine as "Medicinale Anglicum," and so on. The catalogue of the library of the cathedral at Canterbury (1315) has "Regula B. Benedicti glossata Anglice," "Locutio Latina glossata Anglice," "Orationes Anglice," and the like. (Wanley, Pref.) Lambarde published the laws of Ine, Alfred, etc., in 1568, "sermone Anglico;" Dayne printed "The gospels of the fower Evangelistes" in "the vulgar toung of the Saxons," 1571. Camden found (1605) in ancient Saxon glossed Evangelists. The contrivance of the double word seems due to the continental scholars, who must avoid saying English as too modern, and Saxon as likely to be understood of Saxony.

7. Our dictionaries hitherto (1862) do not yet contain all the Saxon English which has been printed. Nor is that ancient tongue limited to type or manuscript. Every word of pure English now spoken by our farmers and husbandmen, every word which can be recovered from old writings, if of true Gothic origin, nay, every homeborn old word used in Iceland, Norway, Sweden, Holland or Germany belongs to us. The speech of northern Europe was once common to all of Skythian breed, and the legend of Seinte Marherete is as good evidence for the English birth of a word, as the Will of Alfred or the Charters of Edgar.

8. I pass on to notice some facts which have reference to our ancient language and its changes. And first, especially, the falling away of N or M at the end of grammatical forms and, sometimes, even of the radical syllable, as when the Man of the Saxon English becomes a little later Me, used where we now put passives. (See Layamon, vol. iii. p. 455.)

9. A living critic (Guest, Philol. Soc. vol. i. p. 151) has hit upon the idea that this Me is the final syllable in Ho-mo, Gu-ma. Let me therefore add, that the Danish and Swedish Men, *but*, becomes

in Early English Me, as in the Ancren Riwle, fol. 101. a, where the editor is quite wrong, in the Legend of St. Catherine of Alexandria, as printed lines 327, 587, 1281. Both these words occur in, Me leof quoð elepsius ʒef me swa biluuede hit were sone iseid þe keiser. (Juliana, fol. 60. a. 9.) But, quoth Elepsius, if one so believed, it would be soon y-said to the kaiser. See here fol. 41. b. 14, fol. 42. b. 12, fol. 45. b. 12. 13, fol. 58. a. 6, fol. 63. b. 10. 11, fol. 64. b. 3. Man is still used in German in the sense given above, the French On all agree is Hom, Homme, and the Saxon English used Man exactly thus, as Matth. vi. 2. Orosius, p. 458. 3. 4, p. 462. 1. 7, p. 464. 21, p. 466. 10, ed. Bohn. Even in the thirteenth century, Man seið þ eise makeð þeof. MSS. Cott. Titus, D.xviii. fol. 117. b. *It is said that opportunity makes the thief.*

10. That the loss of N, M had established itself in our case endings before writings were put on bookfell, is plain enough by comparing Heora *of them* with Latin Eorum *of them*, þæra *of whom* with Quorum *of whom*, Twegra *of two* with Duorum *of two*, Begra *of both* with Am-borum *of both*, Eallra *of all* with Sollorum *of all*, supposing we could find that word, with many others. The genitive plural of the definite declension as Godena was by letter change only different from the indefinite Godra, and the genitives plural of substantives as Gifena had once an M, as †gifenam to be compared with Donorum.

11. Datives singular and plural of demonstrative pronouns and adjectives end in Saxon English and in Mœsogothic in M. In Islandic one of these Ms is lost, namely, from the neuter singular. Of nouns substantive, omitting the declension whose characteristic is -an, we find no dative in M, N acknowledged by the earliest or latest grammars. Yet as in Greek and Latin the declension of adjectives is the same as that of substantives, so, the affinities of our language with those assure us, it must have been with us. Mr. C. W. Goodwin (Guthlac, p. 106) says, " Did the termination -um originally characterize the dative or ablative *singular* of substantives as well as of adjectives ? There is no sense of plurality in such expressions as: on swefnum (see Matth. ii. 22), in a dream ; to gemyndum, to remembrance ; on hys gewealdum, in his power; be lyfum, alive, and many like phrases. It is usual to term -um in these instances, an adverbial termination ; but I see nothing to distinguish it in the examples adduced from a regular

case ending." In the laws of Æþelbirht, ix. all difficulty will be removed by considering Freum as a singular, from Frea, *a lord*; observe a threefold boot is awarded. Pursuing the argument, one hardly can believe we have a plural *milks* in ær þonne þæt acennede bearn fram meolcum awened si. (Beda, 493, 33). Lat. ablactatur. Weallum with mortar. (Genesis, xi. 3.) Getreoþum. (Exod. xxxii. 13.) Gesihðum. (Homil. vol. i. p. 424, line 18.) Gebyrdum at his birth (Homil. vol. i. p. 110) we must regard with the less confidence, because translators often followed their Latin too closely, though Ælfric seems not open to that charge : that Gebyrd is " generally used in the plural " no proof is adduced. The earliest English does not admit the poetical idiom of the Greek and Latin, by which a plural is used to bear the sense of the singular, as Curribus in a 'chariot: they employed however frequently some words in the plural as Rodor, Ceaf, Þystru, Folc, Sælð, Sped. Therefore Hiltum seems to be a singular in Beowulf, 3138. He æfter recede wlat | hwearf þa be wealle | wæpen hafenade | heard be hiltum | Higelaces þegn | yrre and anræd. He looked through the house: then went by the wall Hygelacs thane angry and furious (resolute?) he grasped the weapon hard by the hilt. (Kemble.) A parallel passage is And þa ædre gegrap | sweord be gehiltum (Cædmon, p. 175, last line). *And then hastily gript the sword by the hilt.* Hilt is often sing. Beow. 3347, 3368. Swa hit gedefe bið. | þat mon his winedryhten | wordum herge | ferhðum freoge. Beowulf, end. *As it is fitting that man should extol his friend and lord in words, should love him in spirit.* He gewrac syððan | cealdum cearsiðum | cyning ealdre bineat. Beowulf, 4783. *He punished him afterwards with the cold sorrowful journey* (i.e. *death*), *he deprived the king of life.* (Kemble.) In some instances the vowel has disappeared and the whole of the dative termination has been lost; as Nægled cnearrum, in nailed ships. (Brunanburg battle song, Chronicle, 937.) Æwisc mode. ibid. with mind disgraced, for those who translate Æwisc as nominative plural should prove their construction. Hyrned nebban, with horned neb, ibid. It is not wholly without weight that occasionally the Latin singular is translated by -um, as þeowum þinum for servo tuo, Psalm xviii. 13. Spelman. gyltum delicto, vs. 16. Spelm. On stowum gefryþsumre. In locum munitum, Psalm lxx. 3. Spelm. Sometimes adjectives lose M, as Aȝene sceatte, feo ȝehwilce, LL. Æþelbr. xxx., which Price says is a false concord. Clæne feo, ibid. in the note. Halige martyrdome, Beda, p. 491, line 19, for haligum. Rihte godes dome, Beda, p. 494, line 13, for rihtum. Mid unmæte werode and strange, Beda, p. 499, line 30. Laþlice deaðe, Beda, p. 540, line 1=Detestanda omnibus morte. Mid micle wundre, Beda, p. 544, line 29. Hwylce dage, Beda, p. 579, line 35. Litle weorode, with a little band; in the Brunanburg battle song, Chronicle, 937. Swigende muþe, Beda, p. 512, 13=Ore tacito. Bliþe mode, Beda, p. 598, 43. Hluttre mode, p. 599, 9. Sume dæge, p. 600. 24, p. 610. 10, p. 611. 33. Grimsiende ligum, p. 601. 20. Oðre dæge, p. 605. 30. Forþagane ðy wintre, p. 606. 22, *the winter being gone.* Mid micle wundre, p. 625. 21 (wuldre?). Gehwylce, p. 624. 38. Ealde worde, p. 626. 26, and in other places.

12. From the dative plural the final M sometimes fell away : of the testimony of the MSS. in this case there is no doubt. Hwa þa gyfe sealde. gingum gædelinge. Cædmon, p. 242. 20. *Who those gifts gave to the young comrades.* Gædelinge is here neither an error nor used collectively, but equivalent to Gædelingum, the last letter being dropt. Eallum utagangende, Beda, p. 478, line 10, a plural and for utagangendum. Him forhogiende, Beda, p. 502, line 4, a plural. Swa monigum and swa myclum styrnesse wiþer-weardra ðinga, Beda, p. 646, line 4. Here styrnesse is plural for styrnessum.

13. N occasionally falls away from the third person plural of verbs. I have collected some examples of this in the notes to the Epistola Alexandri ad magistrum suum Aristotelem, page 73. Hæfdon (Beda, p. 502, line 9) and onfenge (line 10) stand in similar conditions. Hi hwurfe (Beda, 506. 41). In the Saxon English Gospels the plural personal terminations often disappear if the pronoun be expressed and follow, as La ȝe for ȝað, ȝelyrbe ȝe for ȝelyrbon, because in these cases the pronoun is concurrent in signification with the termination. But the condition is not a necessary one, þæt hig gelære, Paris Psalter, Ps. ix. 19. A few instances occur here : Hefde for Hefden, fol. 38. a. 11.

14. N had fallen away from the Norse infinitives at an early period. In Seinte Marherete MS. R. but few instances occur, most of the infinitives preserving their Teutonic and Hellenic form. To helpe for To helpen, fol. 42. a. 14. To fordo, fol. 44. b. 22. To loki,

fol. 47. b. 19. The examples Wite waldest for Witen, fol. 50. b. 21, Wite wult, ibid. 22, occur in MS. B. where the rule is to drop the N, as is recorded in our notes. In the Lindisfarne and Rushworth gospels the infinitive has regularly dropped N.

15. N is lost in mi, þi, for min, þin, Seinte Marh., often before consonants: see especially fol. 46. a. 4.

16. M is lost in the dative plural þeo, fol. 38. a. 11, for þeom.

17. N is lost from the past participle iȝeue for ge-gifen, fol. 52. a. 15.

18. E mute does not perhaps appear in this manuscript. þeowe, fol. 37. b. 1, is for þeowa of the older tongue, while þeow, fol. 39. b. 4, is an adjective, and þeowe, fol. 39. b. 6, is the feminine. Wille, fol. 37. b. 6, for Sax. Engl. Willa. Wruhte, Wright, is in Sax. Engl. Wruhta. Bewit, fol. 39. a. 4, as compared with Bewite, fol. 38. b. 20, Wite, fol. 39. a. 8, is either an error of the writer or a rejection of the termination. So of þen, fol. 37. a. 20, with þene, fol. 44. a. 2, and the Saxon English þonne. In fol. 46. a. 16, þrumnesse may be either a way of writing the nominative frequent in Saxon English, which on comparison with the Mœsogothic -nassus appears likely to be as correct as -nes, -nys, or it may be a dative "*in majesty.*" Anfaldte hweðere represents three words Anfald þeh hweðere.

19. Of the decapitation of a word a remarkable instance occurs in Man (fol. 39. a. 19). The Latin of that passage is, Domine, potestas tua non potest ei esse communis. (MSS. Harl. 5327. 2801.) Man therefore is evidently used in the sense of Commune, Communitatem. But Man by itself no more could convey that sense than Munus in Latin; the proper Saxon English for Communis is Gemæne, and the proper Mœsogothic is Gamains. The Ge and Ga in these words are the equivalents in form and sense of the Latin Con, having only lost the N; a part of the word therefore, Con, which was essential to its significance has been dropped. The same thing had happened at an earlier time to the Saxon English word Cweman, which in form is no more than the Mœsogothic Kwiman, our Come, Cuman, but it bears the sense of the Mœsogothic Gakwiman, which answers in both its parts to Convenire; Cweman, however, strictly no more gives the sense of Convenire, than Venire without Con would do; it then has also been beheaded. This Cweman still lives in our Comely, Becoming. The

frequent word Fere *companion*, is also, doubtless, ʒeɟepa, from ʒe
=con, ɟepan=φέρεσθαι=Germ. Fahren, *fare*. See also Man in
the glossary. To all iliche meane (Si sciret, fol. 8. b. 12). *Common
to all alike.* þeo (*they*) beon to alle men oliue iliche meane. (MSS.
Cott. Titus. D.xviii. fol. 118. a. cf. 118. d.) The meyne in alle þing
plesed him next the kyng. (Robert Mannyng of Brunne, p. 68, line
18. *The commonalty gratified him next after the king.*) This is
A.D. 1330: and a similar use may be continually traced till we reach
the MEAN men of our own day. In Cædmon, p. 4, line 11, the
sense *Commonalty* will stand, but in Laws of Ine, p. 54. xxxv. *vile,
false*, unmæne, p. 77. vi. we have another word. Mæne mor, Cod.
dipl. D.xlvi. *the common moor*, the *moor which was common land*.
Mene is similarly employed for *gemein, common* in the Friesic laws.

20. Of letter changes we observe that where þ follows a T or a
D, it becomes T. In the Chronicle after the year 1132 the same
variation may be observed. The last editor of that work is so im-
patient of the change that he has declared the scribe to be "apparently a foreigner." Assimilation in the opposite direction occurs
in the Saxon Gospels, pẏpcẏð þu, Matth. xxi. 23, where neither
edition offers any various reading. In St. Marherete and many
other pieces of the same age And becomes Ant.

21. In this piece, Seinte Marharete, G once or twice takes the
place of þ, as in Wurgen, to worship, fol. 37. b. 4, fol. 40. a. 3, fol.
51. b. 6. 12. Juliana, fol. 67. a. 5, fol. 67. b. 1.

In Layamon also Sir F. Madden writes (Pref. xxxiii.) that H
"as a final . . . . stands for ht and in both texts for ð." There are
many examples in Layamon, of which I note some: biddeh for
biddeþ, line 4134, haldeh for haldeþ, 4136, buh for beoð, 4196,
4206, feorh for forð, 4200, aʒe for aþe, 4259, sohfeste for soþfeste,
4910, worʒ for worþ, 2965, soh for soþ, 3468. 8015. 22975, wih for
wiþ, 7673, deh for doþ, 21482. 20504, mahmes for maðmes, 22399.
The same change may, I think, be seen in WRIGGLE=Dutch
Wriggelen, which is a frequentative of WRITHE = Sax. Eng.
Wriðan, for of that another form Wrig was current and at an early
time recorded. Cf. Dansk. Vrikke, *wriggle*.

> The bore his tayle wrigges
> His rumpe also he frigges
> Against the hye benche.
>   Skelton, Elynour Rummynge, 176.

ON THE LANGUAGE OF ST. MARHERETE. 83

þe deuel wrickede her and þer:'
St. Dunstan, 82, from MS. Harl. 2277.

Also in TARRY which came not direct from Tardare but is the modern representative of an intermediate Targen, since our final Y commonly stands for an older G or Ġ.

& þo he targede a lute while.
St. Kenelm, 179, ibid.

The last example added to those from Layamon makes the proof strongest, since it might be truly alledged that in the Saxon English Wurðian, the significant syllable is Wur, matching Latin Ver-eri, Mœsogothic with sibilation Sweran, and the remainder is but terminations. So also in Wriggle the radical idea lies in WR, answering to Cir-cum etc. Mr. Hardwick would have Wurgan to be Wurðigean. Rask truly lays down that the g in the termination of verbs has the sound of y (art. 200. See note on Orientis Mirab. xxx.), and that this rule is correct is plain from the termination of the Mœsogothic parallel verb in ᏩᎪN : in the 13th century the letter ȝ was in use to express the half consonantal half vowel sound of y, and were Mr. Hardwicks idea carried out the word would be written †wurðȝan. The MS. B. reading fol. 51. b. 6. wurðgan may be thought in some lights to support Mr. Hardwick: but it deserves no weight; thus in the Herbarium, to the contrary, we find Wungynde (vii. 1) written for Wuniende, and not strangely.

22. The change of the gutturals to þ is also so frequent in Layamon, as Worðten for Worhten or Wroughten, line 8711, Broðten for Brohten or Broughten, 9106, Miðte for Mihte or Mighte, 9176, that I have not ventured to alter the MS. reading fol. 50. b. ult. where I take þeines to be aȝeines. Yet since þeo is written (fol. 56. a. 3) for ȝe, it might be proper to correct it as an error.

23. It is acknowledged on all hands that the Saxon English pronoun whose nominative is Se, Seo, þæt, was occasionally used in all its cases as a demonstrative substantive pronoun. In reading soon after publication the last edition 1861 of the Chronicle, I was surprised to see at p. 356, line 3, þeora turned out of the text and heora substituted. This induced me to collect examples of the usage in all cases, numbers, and genders, but a consideration that every reader of our old language, who should not be dreaming over his work, would be fully aware of this, made me lay aside the cita-

M 2

tions. Matth. xxiii. 31, xiii. 19. Looking at the homeric ροί, ραί, ρά, we should expect in the singular †ρός, †ρή, ρό, but proofs are wanting. Editors of the oldest English should not hastily reject, however, whatever traces they find, as þe foresprecena bisceop (St. Guðlac, p. 72), þe haliga Andreas (prose Andreas, p. 18, line 7).

24. The forms SHE, THAT, THEY, THEIR, THEM, with all the other cases now fallen into disuse, were occasionally employed in our language as demonstrative substantive pronouns from the earliest times. In the MS. now before us, þe as nom. sing. masc. is not found, but in St. Cath. MS. Cott. Titus D.xviii. fol. 138. a. þe þ is *He that.* cf. Ancren Riwle, fol. 79. b. : the nom. s. fem. þeo, *she,* occurs in Juliana, fol. 56. b. 6. Ah heo as þeo þ te heouenlich feder luuede. leafde al hire aldrene lahen : *But she, as she that the heavenly father loved, left all her forefathers laws.* Si sciret, fol. 6. a. 1. Juliana, fol. 62. a. 4. Ancren Riwle, fol. 55. a, fol. 71. b. The acc. sing. fem. fol. 38. a. 13. The nom. pl. THEY, þeo, fol. 38. b. 4, fol. 39. b. 12, fol. 44. b. 5, fol. 49. b. 19, fol. 54. a. 22, fol. 53. a. 11. Cath. R. fol. 11. b. 9 = T. fol. 134. a. The dative plural þeo, *to them,* for þeom by loss of M, fol. 38. a. 11. The acc. pl. *them,* þeo, fol. 38. b. 4, fol. 41. b. 9, fol. 47. b. 12, fol. 54. a. 12. 13, fol. 54. b. 5. 12. Si sciret, fol. 2. a. 16. 17, fol. 2. b. 4 bis, fol. 5. b. 20, fol. 7. b. 15, fol. 9. a. 23. Juliana, fol. 56. b. 5. 14, fol. 66. b. 20. 21, fol. 69. a. 6, fol. 68. b. 4. The employment of these forms for the demonstrative was becoming much more common, than in Saxon times, and in the Early English Psalter, perhaps a hundred years later, was fixed almost as in the book English of the present day.

25. This pronoun used as an article is thus declined in the MS. before us, neglecting vowel indifferences.

	M.	F.	N.	Pl.
Nom.	þe	þe	þat, þe	e
Gen.	þes	þer	not found	not found
Dat.	þen	þer	þen	not found
Acc.	þene	þe, þeo	þat, þe	þe

Examples. þe. m. fol. 41. a. 14. þe. fem. fol. 51. a. 21, fol. 51. b. 7. þat. fol. 37. b. 11. 14. þe in MS. Titus D.xviii. = þat in our MS. fol. 3. b. 19. þe meiden. fol. 39. b. 4. þe. plur. fol. 41. a. 12, fol. 42. b. 2. þes. masc. title, fol. 37. b. 13. þer. gen. Si sciret. þer fur, *the fire of it.* fol. 3. a. 21. þen. masc. fol. 38. a. 14. þer. dat. to þer eorðe. fol.

46. b. 15. þen. neut. fol. 47. a. 19 for wiht is either neut. or fem., and unwiht is used neut. þene. fol. 37. b. 21, fol. 44. b. 20, fol. 45. b. 15. þe. fem. fol. 51. a. 17. þeo. to þeo world. Oreison of St. Mary, fol. 70. b. 1. þe. neut. þe sar. fol. 42. b. 3. þe hehe rode taken, fol. 43. a. 8. þat. fol. 52. b. 13. þe. plur. fol. 37. b. 7.

26. In Layamon Sir F. Madden says that "an indeclinable þe is often used before all cases and genders." vol. i. p. xliii. Rather than venture on interpreting the words of another, I prefer to deny the statement, as far as regards the earlier text. It is true that prepositions, which properly governed a dative, are followed by þe instead of the right inflexion. But that is to be accounted for by observing an alteration of the use of prepositions, in which they were followed by the accusative, at least of the article; the cases of pronouns now beginning to show confusion of the dative with the accusative. We have arrived not at þe for the genitive and dative, as well as for the nominative and accusative, but at a change in the idioms of the prepositions. In the MS. now printed, we read Of þat heðene folc, fol. 38. a. 6; the Saxon English Of would govern a dative, but here we have an accusative: so, Of þat lond. fol. 38. b. 4. Of þat an (Si sciret, fol. 10. b. 4). So in Layamon (vol. iii. p. 291), Of þene marmre stane. Toward þat oðer. Si sciret, fol. 10. b. 4. At the same time these prepositions had not wholly laid aside their ancient usage. Adjectives were soon to have the same construction, Hit is ilick þat. MSS. Cott. Titus D. xviii. fol. 117. c.

27. When a genitive comes between the article and the substantive in regimen, an uncertainty about the concord of the article is observable, as in the title MS. B. also fol. 37. b. 12. oþe, oþe, oþes, and it may be taken either to favour Sir F. Madden's view that þe is used as a genitive, or that þe agrees with nome not with faderes, but þes with gastes, or that the writer was puzzled about the concord of an article belonging in fact to two substantives in different cases. In St. Guðlac, p. 2, Mr. Goodwin found þæs arwurðan gemynde Guðlaces, and there was no need to alter it, though þære, as P. 20, also occurs. In John ii. 8. we have þæpe ðpihte ealðpe, in 9. ɼe ðpihte ealðop, where the reprinter wanted to alter þæpe to þam.

28. Unless we limit, more technically than reasonably, the range of our ancient language, we must accept as English every word and every usage, which can be shewn to live in the kindred dialects. Hence substantives admit more genders than one. Wiht, Wuht,

Uht, is sometimes feminine, but neuter as often (Boeth. p. 7, line 19. Oros. p. 464, line 37. ed. Th.); whence we may take here to þen unwiht (fol. 47. a. 19) as neuter. See fol. 42. a. 16, fol. 44. b. 4. Yet þen unsehen unwiht, fol. 44. a. 18, is masc. In St. Marharete the usual genders, with reserve as to the employment of þat, hwet and hit, are preserved for the most part.

29. In the formation of substantives case endings in any vowel are expressed by a final E. A great change appears in the formation of the plural. In Saxon English only masculines like smið would make the nom. acc. plural in -AS, but in the writings we are now considering, first feminines, as Worldes (fol. 55. b. 15), Bokes (fol. 50. b. 11), Mihtes (fol. 52. b. 22), Tunges (Si sciret, fol. 4. a. 9, but Tungen. Titus D.xviii.), Runes (Si sciret, fol. 9. a. 5); secondly neuters, as Wordes (fol. 41. a. 16, fol. 47. a. 2), Hornes (fol. 42. a. 11), Meidenes (fol. 37. b. 20, fol. 42. a. 18), Schrudes (fol. 52. b. 18), Wihtes (fol. 51. b. 13. 15), Werkes (fol. 50. a. 16, fol. 37. a. 22), þinges (fol. 44. b. 3. 6), Wederes (fol. 44. b. 15), Wettres (fol. 44. b. 15), Weoredes (Si sciret, fol. 7. b. 11), are formed on the modern system. On the contrary the ancient rule is observed in Leaf (fol. 37. b. 2), which the Saxon English (Narratiunculæ, fol. 71. b. 11, 12) and the Latin (posui me omnes cartas perlegere, MS. Harl. 2801. fol. xxxiv=63. b.) testify to be plural, and in þing (fol. 44. b. 5). These unlawful plurals appeared in the twelfth century; Huses, Laud MS. of Chron. anno 656. So Fennes. On the fly-leaf of a Cottonian MS. which I have a hope of seeing in print, are twenty lines of twelfth century English, where early examples of some of these changes may be found, thus the feminine Wyrt makes the plural Wyrtas. The modern declension appears also in the genitival S of feminines singular, as Moderes (fol. 38. a. 19), Culures (fol. 42. a. 13, fol. 52. b. 4), Worldes (fol. 50. a. 20), found as early as the Saxon English Gospels (Luke i. 70. Marshal); of words which in earlier times took no termination, as Feaderes (title), Broðeres (fol. 47. b. 10); of words which should make the genitive in n, as Licomes (fol. 37. a. 17); of plurals, as Iweddedes (fol. 43. a. 14), Meidenes (fol. 43. a. 15, fol. 48. b. 19), Monnes (fol. 47. b. 5). In a nearly cotemporary writing we have our WHOSE put, to break a Saxons heart, as a plural, Engles hwas felahes ha beoð. MSS. Cott. Titus, D.xviii. fol. 117. c. *Angels whose fellows they be.* The expression is as shocking as would be †oxes for Oxen, †hoses for Hosen.

ON THE LANGUAGE OF ST. MARHERETE.   87

30. Some genitives in -ene for Saxon English -ena are also met with. These are found regularly in the Saxon AN declension, and in a very few feminines. Sawlene (fol. 41. b. 7) was before Sapla, Englene (fol. 45. b. 11) was Enʒla, Kingene was Cẏnınʒa; but Widewena (fol. 43. a. 14), Reuene (fol. 52. a. 6) have followed the older formation, only changing A into E. It must not however be confidently assumed that Saplena, Enʒlena, Kınʒena were never used; perhaps they are the true older genitives; and we know certainly of some instances in which -ena, -a were interchangeable, as Beda, p. 628, line 23. Dagena, Paris Psalter, Ps. lxxvii. 32. Comparison of other tongues allied to our own would suggest that as Deum=Deorum=†deonum, so the proper termination of the plural genitive with us had once been -enam, then by loss of N, -ena, then by contraction -a.

31. Many of these alterations of the language are found in the gloss upon the Lindisfarne Gospels. Bouterwek (p. clix. seqq.) has collected a list: thus modern plurals, Cægas, Keys, fem. Costunges, fem. Burgas, Boroughs, fem. Ebolsungas, fem. Culfras, Culvers, fem.; modern genitives Brydgumes, Bridegrooms, Intinges, Lichomes, which once ended in -an, Ældes, Æs, Brydes, Ceastres, Portcuoenes, Cirices, Dedes, Eorðes, Gefes, Hæles, Heartes, Helles, Lufes, Mæhtes, Moderes, Rodes, Saules, Synnes, Tunges, Woruldes, which as feminines could not in the older language take a final S. There is also a long list of feminines of other forms. Genitives in -ana, which would not usually be so formed in all that we know of the oldest English, whether masculines, feminines, or neuters, are also numerous in the Lindisfarne Gloss. Bouterwek gives (pp. clxii, clxiii) a list in which most of the formations are unusual. Were the deviation confined to genitives plural in*-ena it would be easy to set the difference down to dialect, but it is necessary to go back to a very high antiquity, long before Hengist and Horsa, for masculines and feminines making the genitive singular both in -S. Sir Frederick Madden has dated the Lindisfarne Gloss at 950; two hundred and fifty years earlier than this piece of St. Marherete, and as early as the greater part of our Saxon English literature. The internal evidence seems strongly against this date, and upon that, I suppose, or that chiefly, Bouterwek, who must have spent a good deal of time upon his book, whatever his real merits may be, gives his opinion that the

Lindisfarne Gloss was introduced about the middle of the twelfth century, or about fifty years from the probable date of St. Marherete. (Vielleicht erst gegen die Mitte des 12 Jahrh. jedenfalls nicht vor dem J. 1104, wurde von einem Presbyter Aldrêd die nordhumbr. Interlinearglosse in den Codex eingetragen. p. xlvii.) All these variations from the older model are also found in Layamon (A.D. about 1206).

82. The datives in -um dwindle to -e, except in phrases like our SELDOM, which had become adverbial, as Lytlen and lytlen (fol. 47. a. 18).

33. In the same manner the terminations of adjectives in the definite construction become -e, as te wilde deor, on þeos wilde waldes (fol. 44. b. 17), þene acursede gast (21).

34. In old English au adjective is oftener used as a substantive than in these later days; so in the Saxon Gospels, Matthew xii. 29, 45. Marshal. Bolde, *a bold man*, Brown, *brown deer*, Gawaine and Grene Knight, 21, 1162. Crewelle, *cruel man*, Aunturs of Arthur, xlviii. Wari, St. M. fol. 39. b. 15.

35. The pronouns are thus declined:—

	Sing.	Dual.	Plur.
Nom.	I=I'=Ic=Ich		We
Gen.	Min, Mi	not found	Ure
Dat. Acc.	Me	not found	Us

The gen. Min occurs after the preposition Of (fol. 43. b. 5). Mi, Ure only where they may be called adjectives.

36.

	Sing.	Dual.	Plur.
Nom.	þu		ʒe
Gen.	þin	incker (Si sciret, fol. 10. a. 11).	ower
Dat. Acc.	þe	inc (fol. 54. b. 20).	ow

The genitives where they occur may be called adjectives, even in the expression þin anes help (fol. 61. a. 20), *help of thee only*.

37.

	Sing. M.	Sing. F.	Sing. N.	Plural.
Nom.	He	Ha, Heo	Hit	Ha, Heo
Gen.	His	Hire		Hare
Dat. Acc.	Him	Hire		Ham, Heom
Acc.		Ha (fol. 41. b. 18).		

We still retain HE, IT, HIS, HER, HIM, HER, EM. Its is a modern word.

The other demonstrative has been considered above.

38. We observe an early appearance of the modern use, by which grammatical genders being forgotten, the pronouns begin to refer to sex. No language perhaps ever refused to construct according to signification rather than form, but we have now a wide departure from the method of Saxon English in the use of the neuter Hit with antecedents masc. and fem. Þat also is made to stand as demonstrative, call it pronoun, call it article, as you will, with masculines and feminines, and it is plain enough from some of the examples, out of no confusion of genders of nouns but as we now say THAT man, forgetting the history of That, not the masculine sense of Man. Hit refers to the masc. Wil (fol. 41. a. 3), to Stench (Si sciret, fol. 3. a. 18), to Stream (fol. 44. b. 14), to Blosme (fol. 39. a. 3, 5 bis, 8), to Eoli (fol. 46. a. 1)—but that word though masc. in English (Matth. xxv. 3. Beda, p. 541, l. 31, 34) is neuter in Mœsogothic, Latin and Hellenic,—to Seam (Juliana, fol. 66. b. 8) : to the feminines Bitternesse (fol. 40. b. 11), Hude (fol. 51. b. 22), Milce (fol. 53. b. 4), Blisse (Si sciret, fol. 9. b. 14), Behest (fol. 40. b. 6). A passage of the translation of Beda (p. 616, line 12) in which the feminine (p. 616, line 4) blodlæswu is followed by Hit may be supposed an example of this idiom, but in writing Hit, the translator was rather thinking of the action, which would rightly be given by a neuter. Wund which is feminine is followed by Hyt (Herbarium, iv. 8), pynt f. by Hyt, v. 7, but the writer had in his thoughts the act of applying the remedy: thus in the Herbarium frequently; but yet we find there some passages which without harshness can only be constructed so that Hit shall refer to a previous not neuter antecedent, as i. 15. THAT refers to the masculines Time (fol. 53. a. 2), Stude (fol. 44. a. 8), Gra (fol. 44. a. 15, fol. 46. a. 20), Wurm (fol. 45. b. 22), Man (Juliana, fol. 64. b. 2), Grisliche, *Grisly one* (Jul. fol. 65. a. 1), to Hird (fol. 56. a. 8. Si sciret, fol. 1. a. 14, fol. 6. b. 9, fol. 10. a. 18); the Saxon Hired is masc., as in Psalm xxi. 28. hıɲeðaɾ, and in Job. init. micelne hıɲeð; to Read (fol. 42. a. 6), to Stream (fol. 42. a. 22) ; to the feminines þeosternesse (Si sciret, fol. 3. b. 1), Wildernesse (Jul. fol. 62. b. 11), Culure (fol. 52. b. 20), Unselhðe (fol. 43. b. 21), to Reowðe (fol. 52. a. 2), which may be presumed feminines. Hwet Godd also is found (fol. 39. b. 6).

39. To this usage such passages as Nis þæt seld guma wæpnum geweorðad (Beowulf, 496) should not be referred but to such an idiom as Hit ic eom, It am I, nor should such a passage be turned "That man is not one," but "That is not a man." The change of gender in Ines law lxxv. is hardly an example. The fly-leaf above mentioned (art. 29) has Leg siððen þæt wyrt, where Wyrt is feminine and Lege is the regular imperative for *Lay.* To a late date (A.D. 1100 ?) belongs the Nathanis Iudæi Legatio, which exhibits þæt aðle for seo aðl, but ðæt aðl is also found in the parallel passage of St. Veronix which is said to be at least not lower than 1050 A.D.

40. We observe also the modern use of THAT as a relative pronoun with antecedents of all genders and numbers, always standing first in its clause, never preceded even by a preposition. Instances may be seen everywhere in Seinte Marherete. Two or three examples in that English, which we call Saxon, occur in Orientis Mirabilia, § xxvii. In the translation of Rask's Grammar (art. 153) on the relative force of the declinable ſe, ſeo, þæt, the first example would seem to an unsuspicious student, misled by Thorpes translation, to furnish an instance of this idiom; hatan þæt sælþa, þæt nåne ne beoð, which we find loosely modernized, *to call those blessings which are none*; the construction is *Id felicitatem appellare, quod nulla sit felicitas*; or as Rask gave it with entire correctness (p. 44) *Kalde det Lyksaligheder som ingen* (*Lyksaligheder*) *er.* The last entries in the Chronicle use þæt in the same way. In mani of þe castles wæron lof and grim. Þ wæron rachenteges. Þ twa other thre men hadden onoh to bæron onne (p. 382, line 30). *In many of the castles were Love (?) and Grim which were chains, of which two or three men had enough to do to bear one.* (So line 34, p. 383. 25. The translator is absurd. In p. 383. 13, the author meant *he had it roofed.*) In Æþelstans Dooms, p. 87. ix, þæt is translated *who* with a masc. antecedent, but without necessity. In Laws, p. 100, line 7, þæt may at first sight seem to have a feminine antecedent, but another construction is possible.

41. The inflexions of adjectives in St. Marherete are mostly reduced to -e, see fol. 52. b. 9 : yet we have Anes, Nanes, Ane, Hire ane (fol. 42. a. 9), Minne, þinne (fol. 63. b. 13), þisne (fol. 65. b. 9). The termination in -re, common in Layamon, does not appear in Seinte Marharete ; Of nane sikernesse (fol. 6. a. 10). The dative

plural is Bi ham ane (fol. 48. a. 13). Anes is found constructed about this time with feminines þin anes (MSS. Cott. Titus, D.xviii. fol. 120. c.) and with plurals (ibid. fol. 121. b. 1).

42. Besides the ancient relative þe, which, let me say by the way, is probably the declinable relative Se, Seo, þæt,=Qui, Quæ, Quod, divested of case endings, and in that way a sort of anticipation of the demonstrative modern THE, we have a new set of relatives introduced into the language and beginning with HW, as Hwen, *When* (fol. 41. b. 21), Hwas, *Whose* (fol. 44. b. 1), Hwer, *Where* (fol. 45. a. 21). They are frequent in the MS. before us. The older tongue knew these only as interrogatives and indefinites, for though Ælfric (Gram. p. 21, line 29) call quis=hwa a relative, he is mistaken both in his logic and his Latin, in his example it is interrogative and the Latin should be Quis hoc fecerit. The only instance, which has caught my eye, of Hwæt taken relatively, in early Saxon English, is in St. Swiðhun (p. 2, facsimile, line 21), Sæbe þa be enðebyrðnysse hwæt Swiðhun him bebeád. *He said then in order what S. him bade.* Mr. Earle puts his text of St. Swiðhun at A.D. 985. The Lindisfarne Gloss has these forms as relatives, but I regard that as of late date. Ælfric in the page just named (line 13) translates Quæ, Quod by Hwilc. In the MS. before us Hwuch is used in its proper and peculiar sense=Mœsogothic Hwileiks=Latin Qualis, *What like*, Telle us hwuch is helle (Si sciret, fol. 3. a. 11), *Tell us what like is hell* (so fol. 4. b. 15). The last editor of Alfreds laws (p. 36, note) calls Hwelcne a relative where it is indefinite; this seems to be from ignorance of general grammar.

43. Among the old idioms of our tongue, lies almost concealed, one of which our grammarians seem to have no idea. Rask, who was a good general linguist, says, "This language having no passive form" (258.), which is not quite true; I propose to show that the language has traces of a passive. In the Mœsogothic one way of obtaining a passive was the insertion of N after the radical letters of the active (Massmann, p. 808, with fifty-two examples), and this may be detected in the English of the earliest writings. In St. Marherete we have the verb Lear, *to teach*,=Germ. Lehren = Mœsog. Laisyan = Sax. Engl. Læran; the passive of this is LEARN, which our fathers tongue, welling up ever from its deep sheer springs, has given us since the age of bookish Ælfric. There

was a time when this verb was confounded with its original active; "Lead me forth in thy truth and learn me." Psalm xxv. 4. DROWN, in Saxon English Druncnian (an MS. in Lye, Matth. xxiv. 30. Druncnia in the Lindisfarne Gospels), here also (fol. 52. a. 19, fol. 49. b. 7.), *mergi*, is the passive of Drencian, to Drench; this Drown is now made also active. To Bet, with E long, still lives in our homely talk, and means *to make good*, whence a substantive Boot, now almost lost, except in the phrase "to boot," "bootless," *good-less, profitless*, also comparative adjective Better, superlative Best: of this the passive appears here in St. Marherete and once in the passive sense (fol. 55. b. 2); this also passed into an active (fol. 37. b. 7). BURN coming from the root Fÿp, Fire, Πυρ must have been properly a passive; its active form of the weak conjugation Bæpnan must be secondary to this passive and the true active must be lost in English: it once existed in Hellenic as †πυρεναι forming the participial substantive Πυρετος for †πυρεντος, and has been perhaps detected in Latin as Vrere for †burere, Comburere. Rask's doctrine about the different vocalization is a mere delusion of his own. (See Beda, p. 548. 25.) Awæccan *suscitare*, Awæcnian *suscitari* is so plain that we may well wonder it has not been remarked. This N may very probably be a remnant of the past participle, which usually has a passive sense; a supposition, which would account for the change of vowel in Botnian, for the substantive shows that the original verb was Betan, †beat, †boten: certainly "gut, nützlich machen" not "sein."

44. Before dismissing the verb passive I will take one more instance, in which I must appeal to languages not Gothic. Our word Mourn, ⱮuƿnaN, Mœsogothic MAꟽKNAN, answers to and is used by Ulfilas to translate Μεριμνᾶν, which comes from Μέριμνα, which again is a participial substantive from a root Mer-: if we regard this monosyllable as containing the sense *Vex*, then the English and Gothic have a passive N and mean *be vexed*: nor does the Latin forbid; for though Mœrere seems to call upon us to assign a neuter sense to the radix, Mœstus on the other hand is content with an active. The signification *vex* belongs in the Hebrew to the syllable Mar, which the lexica translate by *mœrore affecit*. Our Mar, myƿnan, ⱮIƿnaN, meƿnaN has a much less clear approach to that meaning.

45. Reflexive verbs have a reflexive sense, so in Hellenic Κόπ-

τεσθαι, *to chop oneself*, *to beat ones breast*, Λέγειν, *to Lay*, Λέγεσθαι, *to Lay oneself, to Lie*. Reciprocal verbs are those which express a reciprocated action, as Ἀσπάζεσθαι, *to embrace and be embraced*. Ælfric in his grammar (p. 22, line 51) has a better knowledge on the subject than is everywhere current now. On þam worde bið ægþer ge dæd. ge ðrowung. Osculor te. Ic cysse ðe. et Osculor a te. and Ic am fram þe cyssed. *In the verbs in -or is either the deed or the throe-ing, the active or the passive sense, either I kiss thee or I am by thee kissed*. Complector te. Ic ymbclippi ðe. et complector a te. and Ic eom fram þe ymbclipped. *I embrace thee and I am by thee embraced*. The reciprocal sense in Seinte Marharete is expressed by a reflexive form as is the case in many Latin and Hellenic verbs; but as in modern French it is done by calling in a pronoun: the old method once common no doubt to us with the Romans and Pelasgians, that is, by the heavier termination, is lost to our language. Luuien ham (fol. 48. a. 10), *to love one another*, Seon ham (fol. 49. b. 2), *see one another*. So, Hy custen ham a stounde (The Geste of Kyng Horn, 743), *they kissed one another*: þan eiþer hent oþer hastely in armes | And wiþ kene kosses kuþþed hem togidere. (William and the Werwolf, fol. 15.) *Then either held other hastily in arms, and with keen kisses they cuddled em together, treated one another as familiars*: ȝe hondleð op (MS. Cott. Titus, D.xviii. fol. 117. a.), *you handle one another*. Me þeo þ best luuieð ham (ib. fol. 121. c.), *But they who best love one another*.

46. The irregularity of the verb Witan, *to know*, which makes in the present, 1. Ic wat, I wot, 2. þu wast, 3. He wot, has been explained by the German scholars. The verb originally meant *see*, Ἰδεῖν, Videre, and because I saw is the same thing to a practical man as I know, the past tense of Witan *to see* came to signify *I know*. The verb Witan in Seinte Marherete is often used for *guard, protect*, and is a trace of the old sense *see*, and *see to*, which is found occasionally in the earlier English (Lye) and must have been more familiar in common speech than in books, whence it has at length found its way into these writings. Another irregular Teutonic verb may be explained in the same manner, and it shews, I think, that there still live in our talk words which are far older than their derivatives in Homeros or Lucretius. Ken in the North means *see*, the past tense Kan, Can would therefore mean *I saw*, hence *I know* as it does in Saxon English. Ken, *see*, is therefore

the ancient root of Γνῶναι, Nosse for †gnosse, still preserved among ourselves. In the same manner as I wot is an ancient præterite used as a new present; so Οἶδα, *I know*, is also a præterite, but not as Greek grammars ignorantly and presumptuously teach us, from an old present of the same sense, but from the lost Hellenic equivalent of Video, *I see*, so that Οἶδα was once †*I have seen*, before it was *I know*.

47. The verb Witan once=Videre, præt. Wat=Vidi, part. past Witen=†vid-tus, being put upon a new footing and its past tense being treated as a present, acquired wrongfully and anomalously a new præterite pıꞅte, as, ȝef þe husebonde wiste (subj.), Si sciret paterfamilias (fol. 1. a. 6), with, in the MS. we are examining, an anomalous participle past I wist (fol. 1. b. 7, fol. 38. a. 11).

48. In the strong conjugation of verbs the 2nd person sing. of the præterite had no st, and this had not been altered in the beginning of the thirteenth century; thus we find, þu com me to helpe. feng to fihte for me (Wooing of Jesus, fol. 130. a.), þu cheas (ib. b.). Hence Wast and Canst, Canest (Layamon, Ormulum), Const (Beow. 2748), Cost, are in breach of the rule.

49. The conjugation of the verbs would doubtless have interest, but probably would draw on a discussion inconveniently wide. One point however must be remarked. As the strong form in many verbs, such as Help, Holp, Holpen, has given-way to the weak one, Help, Helped, Helped, we look for examples. Even as early as the date 1052 in the Chronicle Gepyrpte for ȝepeaꝑp is discovered in a passage which the translator sadly mangled (p. 320, line 30). Thus we find here Drehde subj. præt. for Drohe (fol. 52. a. 19, var. read. on fol. 38. b. 1) or Dreahe, Schuptest (fol. 53. b. 4) for Scope, Hehte for Hat. Similar instances have been observed in Layamon by its editor (Gramm. Anal. p. l.), among these Scop and Scupte both in use. In our earliest literature we see ꝼoꝃ and ꝼeꝃðe, Holen and Heled, Eced and Eacen, between which there is no difference, but that of inflexion.

50. The old use of the present form for future time, seems in this MS. to be not discoverable. The genuine potential and subjunctives are frequent, as pres. fol. 52. a. 7, fol. 55. b. 17, fol. 53. a. 18, fol. 40. b. 1. præt. fol. 52. a. 8. 19, fol. 53. a. 19, with the true consequence of the tenses. These parts of the old conjugation are still known to us: Would that it were so!=*Vellem ita esset*: To

do unto others as I would they should do unto me, *quemadmodum vellem*, not *volui*.

> Say this were death
> That now hath seized them: why they were no worse
> Than now they are.
>
> Tempest, Act ii. Scene 1.

But not all the phrases cited above could be expressed in the English of today without auxiliary verbs. Do and Did as mere auxiliaries are quite unknown in the twelfth century.

51. The change of all the final þorns of the verb, of the third singular as Haueð=Habet, of the plural as Haueð=Habemus, Habetis, Habent, of the plural imperative Haueð=Habete into S, is not found in this MS.: though it appears close upon this date, and is seen even in the Lindisfarne Gloss, which if not so old as 950 is at least older than 1200. Thus Foxas holas habbas. Matth. viii. 20. *Foxes have holes.* Ge infindas asal gebunden and fola mið hia unbindas and tolædas me. xxi. 2. *Ye will find ass bound and foal mid her, unbind and to me lead*, in the glossed gospels.

52. Of the second person singular the T is preserved, while it disappears occasionally in Thwaiteses text of the Pentateuch and constantly in the late Saxon English gloss of the Psalter (MSS. Cott. Vesp. A. i.) published by the Surtees Society; as, For hwon ðu asagas rehtwisnisse mine and genimes cyðnisse mine ðorh muð ðinne. Psalm xlix. 16. *For what a-sayest thou my rightwiseness and nimest my revelation through thy mouth?* Layamon, 8307.

53. The pronoun Thou makes one word with its verb if preceding it, as Heiestu, fol. 39. b. 7, Leuestu, fol. 39. b. 10, Felestu, fol. 42. b. 6. We find Willtu in Beda, p. 616, line 30, in a conversation, familiarly: Wastu, p. 630, line 1, Onfehstu, line 27.

54. The grammars by Rask and others do not state what is the third person imperative; in verbs of the strong conjugation the second person has no accidental termination, but the third has usually -e, so that Nim is *take*, Nime *let him take*. The irregularity of Bide has been examined in Orientis Mirabilia, p. 83. Wite, which occurs several times here, is perhaps to be explained as an archaism, for it represents Fίδεθι, the true original form of ἴδε. Of the third person Scott has made familiar one example.

> Woe worth the chase, woe worth the day,
> That costs thy life, my gallant grey!
>
> Lady of the Lake, Canto i.

55. Adverbs lean to the ending -es, as Togederes, fol. 50. b. 13. 19, fol. 43. a. 1. So a northcountryman will now say Somewheres, Anywheres. This is probably an approximation to the older Nihtes, *by night*, Dages, *by day*.

56. The pronoun Ic, Ich, sometimes becomes I without the accent of emphasis and coalesces with the verb. Examples may be collected by comparing the text with the modern equivalent.

57. Prepositions often lose the final N and join themselves to the next word. Examples are of constant occurrence; see the same thing in the Index to Layamon, for instance verse 12788.

58. It is said that Kembles transcripts of the charters are not to be trusted for faithful reproductions of the records: else one might remark that down to 1066 little change had taken place in our language since Ælfred englished as much as seemed to him good, of Orosius; the early charters are always open to alteration by later hands, which without a thought of bad faith used words and inflexions according to the custom of their own times, and the great body of our earliest literature dates little before A.D. 1000. Taking Ælfred as our guide in his Orosius, we should, even making some allowances for Kembles grammatical prejudgements, say, that looking at dated documents no great change in English from that king down to the Conquest can be detected. One hundred and fifty years later, as in St. Marherete, a vast difference is discoverable at first sight. Between that and our modern mode how many have been the variations! How many the pure old English words wholly unknown to educated men of the present day!

Vt silvæ foliis pronos mutantur in annos
Prima cadunt ; ita verborum vetus interit ætas.

Q. H. F.

GLOSSARY.

N.B. Only the more uncommon words are here given.

BLAMON, *Æthiopian.* fol. 45. b. 2. Qui sedit ut homo niger. MS. Harl. 5327. fol. 17. b. Sedentem velut hominem nigrum. MS. Harl. 2801. fol. 64. Bleómannes berge. Codex dipl. ccc. *the negros barrow*: Efter þreottene ȝer com þe akursede gost þet hefde hire itented blac ase a bloamon and bigon to greden. Ancren Riwle, fol. 62. b. Blamon. Cleop. C.vi. fol. 101. b. Swartere þan eni bloman. MS. Harl. 2277. fol. 113. b. Mid him com moni Aufrican ./ of Ethiope he brohte þa bleomen. Layamon, v. 25381. Bláland, *Æthiopia vel tota Africa.* B.H. Blamand, *blackamoor,* Danish. Cf. fol. 43. a. 3. Blues. Blá means *blue,* and I do not see why this description applies to the Æthiopians; but incline to think that it is an adaptation of Blemmyes, who, with the Nubians, came into notice five or six centuries after our era, (Priscus, p. 153, line 16. Corp. Hist. Byz.) instead of Æthiopians.

BISTAÐED, *bestead,* fol. 39. a. 12. Ancren Riwle, fol. 71. a. Juliana, fol. 60. b. 10, fol. 61. a. 15.

CNURNEDE, *gnarred, gnarled.* fol. 45. b. 3. Knorre, *Tuber, tuberculum, nodus, clavus.* Kilian: etymologically related to Knot, Nodus for †gnodus, Knag. Stretching forth his fingers in sight and all about, Without knot or knor or any sign of gout. Hist. of Beryn. 1780. Seldom has there been a face more gnarled and knotted with crabbed cogitation. Southeys Doctor.

COPNI, *I expect, await.* fol. 54. b. 2. pres. first p. sing. A word formed by adding a (no longer passive) N to the Saxon English, Cepan, *observe,* as Homil. vol. i. pp. 484. 524. 580 bis. Ower glade wreond ower cume ikepeð. Ancren Riwle, fol. 49. a. *Our glad friend our coming awaiteth.* For ich iseo ihū crist þe copneð ant cleopeð me. St. Cath. fol. 35. b. þe wunnunge of euch wunne kepeð ant copneð þi cume. fol. 36. a. *The abode of each joy awaiteth and watcheth for thy coming.* Copneð ant kepeð hwuch ure is kempe

o

to ouercumen oðer. fol. 19. a. With gopnyng of þat ilke gomen, þat gostlych speked | With his hede in his honde before þe heȝe table. Sir Gawayne and the Grene Knyȝt, 2461. The Latin is, Constanter certa, beata Margareta, quam chorus omnium sanctorum tuum præstolatur aduentum. MSS. Cott. Calig. A. viii.

Cost, *chosen.* fol. 43. a. 4. The verb Choose, Chose, Chosen= Ceosan, Ceas, Coren (with S changed to R) is of the strong conjugation, but I have elsewhere shewn, that all participles active and passive in the oldest times ended in -ent, -end, and Cost, Coren are both forms of †cosent: ȝecoſt, *probatus, tried,* occurs Lib. Med. i. 45. Paris Psalter, Ps. lxvii. 27. The Latin Gustus is a participial substantive formed on the same root, and in the same manner as Cost. There can be little doubt but that Chew, Γεύεσθαι, Cheek, which means *maxilla,* Jaw, Jowl and many others are of the same family. Cust fem. in the Heliand, *electio* etc. *selectissima quæque,* is another participial substantive. In Beowulf, Kemble, referring probably to Schmeller, puts down Cyst as fem. *excellentia,* but that would hardly answer the construction þæt wæpna cyst (line 3112), for surely he did not hold with the exploded doctrine that the neuter þæt may be constructed with feminines, nor would he probably anticipate the idiom of 1200 A.D. (art. 38). Cyst in that place of Beowulf is a neuter participle, being in construction with a neuter substantive.

Wesseaxe forð.
Onðlongne dæg. eorod cistum.
on last legdun. laþum þeoðum.
Chron. anno 937, p. 202. 28.

The West Seaxe for a long day with the troop chosen ones laid the last on the loathed nations. In Cædmon, p. 188. 32, p. 192. 10. 11, a substantive must be used, and Lye (under Tir) with others takes it as *Caterva, Band,* but the origin of the substantive remains the same: Legio is from Legere, *to pick, choose,* and always military service rejects the lame, the blind, the deaf, the old, the weak. Though the above account of the word seems better supported, there exists, however, a possible origin in Ceaſt, *contention,* with the Friesic Káse, *contention, strife, massacre, fight.*

Cost, *canst,* fol. 50. b. 10, is like Wost for Woldest in the later text of Layamon, 16034; Sost for Soldest, 18747. The rejection of M, N, not to say other letters, before other consonants is very familiar to those who trace out words through different languages. In Somersetshire they say Caznt for Canst thou not.

CRENCHEN UT, *to crane out.* fol. 44. a. 13. Cf. the German Kranich, *a crane*: in Saxon English we only know as yet Crán.

DIUERI, *sorrowful.* fol. 50. b. 13. *Onager tristitiæ* is translated feldhasser of dyernes. Apology for the Lollards, p. 58, line 13. þat ha ne schulden nowðer diueren ne dreden. St. Cath. Titus, fol. 137. b. And tu þat al þe world fore mihte drede and diuere; (Wooing of our Lord, fol. 132. a.) *Thou for whom all the world might dread and grieve.* In this last very near to Dither.

DRIUEL, *drudge.* fol. 51. b. 20. Te deouel hwaȝ driueles ȝe beoð. Juliana, fol. 60. b. 10. þes deoules driueles, fol. 67. a. 21. As þes deoules driueles drohen to fordon hire. St. Cath. MS. Reg. 17. A. xxvii. fol. 33. a. Mare beon idrecchet þen eni driuel. Hali Meidenhad, fol. 120. d. Drevel, *mediastinus*, et *servus*, Anglice Drivil (Kilian). Dribble, *a servant*, generally joined with the epithet true, "He's a true dribble," laborious and diligent (Carrs Craven Glossary, and so Ray). Tusser (p. 318. ed. Mavor=197. Southeys Poets) uses the word in a bad sense, but still for *servants.*

By such like evils I saw such drivels
To come to naught.

This word has the adjectival -ol suffixed, it seems, to Drive, in the sense Drive a trade: Wirthschaft treiben, *cauponariam tractare*, blutschande treiben, *exercere incestum*, durchtrieben, *valde exercitatus* are cited by Wachter; ther tha wald drifth, *who drives the wield, exercises the power*, thet thu nen falsk witscip ne driue, *that thou drive no false witness*, by Richthofen.

DRUPI, *troubled.* fol. 50. b. 13. Cf. Dutch Droevig, *sad, sorrowful.* Low German Dröve, Drövt. Mœsogothic Draibyan, *to vex*, σκύλλειν. Darede al adeadet durcninde and dreori ant drupest alre monne. St. Cath. fol. 32. a. *Damaged all adeaded darkening and dreary and drupest of all men.* Ant makieð drupie chere. Ancren Riwle, fol. 21. Droupy and drowsy, Scurvy and lowsy. Skelton, Elynour Rummynge, 15.

DUHTI, *doughty, worthy*, fol. 43. a. 11, related to Dignus, perhaps to Decet, Saxon English Dugan, Duguð: the full Duhtiȝ has not yet been found.

Dung, *a deep.* fol. 49. b. 7.
   Gewitan him þa Norþmen. nægled cnearrum.
   Dreorig daraða laf. on dinges mere.
   Chron. anno 937.

Away went the Northmen in nailed barks, a dreary darts leaving on the dungs mere: that is, on the sea pool; the "quite conjectural" rendering lately published confesses itself groundless. Ha beoð so wise þat ha witen alle Godes runes. ant his reades þat derne beoð ant deoppre þen eni sea dingle. Si sciret, fol. 9. a. 5. *They be so wise that they know all Gods secrets and his redes, that be concealed and deeper than any sea dingle.* In the Karlsruhe Gloss. p. 161. Gurgitem, Tunculle. By letter change Dump, *a deep hole in water feigned at least to be bottomless.* (Grose.) German Dumpfel, *a deep place in a river or lake; a deep puddle, pool*; in den gemeinen Mundarten Ober- und Niederdeutschlandes eine tiefe stelle in einem Flusse oder See. (Adelung). By throwing off the liquid, A Dub, *a pool of water.* Bor. (Bishop Kennets Collections Lansdowne MSS. 1033. Grose.) Cf. the Low German Dobbe. In the following passage, Teke þis heo mote ȝete þuruh hire uorbisne ant þuruh hire holi beoden ȝiuen oðre strenðe. ant upholden ham þet heo ne uallen iðe dunge of sunne. Ancren Riwle, R. fol. 36. a. *To eke this, she may yet through her example and through her holy prayers give others strength and uphold them that they ne fall in the dung of sin,* though the sense *abyss* appear better, another MS. (Titus) has fulðe, *filth.* With these words relating to water we must connect Dingle, Draytons Dimble (Polyolb. ii.) and Groses Dumble, *a woody valley* (Supplement), of the same thing on the land. My previous conjecture of a connexion with Βέρθος, Βάθος, Βύσσος, a sibilate equivalent, and Τέμπεα seems confirmed. Students of words with their changes will not reject, "A Bumby, *a deep place of Mire and Dung, a filthy Puddle.*" (Ray).

Duuelunge, *in sinking.* fol. 54. a. 4. Def duuelunge dun to þer eorðe. Jul. fol. 69. b. 9. Ah felle ba for fearlac dun duuel rihtes. St. Cath. 1598.

Eawl, *an awl, a fork, an instrument of torture.* fol. 42. a. 3. *ungulis*, MS. Harl. 5327, fol. 11. b. apul, *fuscinula*, Ælf. Gram. p. 6, line 54. *subula, harpago, tridens, a shoomakers awle, a forke, a fire-forke, a flesh hook.* Somner. The same word as ȝeafl which is an instrument of torture in Homil. vol. i. p. 430. Tuhen hire tittes up of hire breosten bi ðe bare bane wið eawles of irne. St. Cath. Titus, fol. 145. d. *Tugged her tittes up from her breast by the bare bone with eawls of iron.* þe deoflen schulen pleien mid ham. mid hore scharpe aules. Ancren Riwle, fol. 56. a. *The devils shall play with them with their sharp awls.*

EGEDE, *stupid.* fol. 45. b. 19. Understonden hwu lutel wurð is prude and hwu egede þing is horel (oŋʒel), Ancren Riwle, fol. 76. a. translated *Stolida.* þat hit þunche egede. Hali Meidenhad, fol. 123. c. *That it seems stupid.* The word seems to have passed from the sense *awestruck* to that of *stupid.* Eggyñ, as toþe for sowre mete. *Obstupeo.* Promptorium Parv. See Onegæn in Lye.

ENDE, *a district.* fol. 50. a. 10. masc. Eallne þone east ende. Chron. p. 316, line 31. Ofer ealne þisne norð ende. ib. p. 314, line 17. On ælcum ende mines anwealdes. Laws, p. 116, line 18. In all these passages the translator has shewn his ignorance of the word. Si aucuns uescunte u prouost mesfait as humes de sa ende. Laws, p. 201, line 24. If any viscount or provost has wronged men of his End: where the editor wants to substitute Baillie, *bailiwick*, out of the Latin equivalent. Schaltu na lengere leuen in ure ende. Si sciret, fol. 10. a. 8. Layamon, 17231. 30398. 11648. We may, I suppose, trace the word in Lord Braybrookes seat, Audley End, in the Dale End district of Birmingham, in Ponders End on the Eastern Counties Railway. It may also perhaps be discoverable in the Andheafod of the Codex Diplomaticus. The Mœsogothic spells with A, And-. The same sense is found in the old Friesic. Da bisette ellick syn oerd ende syn end (Richthofen), *then let each occupy his place and his end*; in the Enti of the old high German, as, fuor in thiu enti tyri und sydonis. Graff. vol. i. col. 356. *the borders of Tyre and Sidon.* In the passages of the old English Gospels, as Matth. xv. 21. 39, xix. 1. Mark, vii. 24, x. 1. ed. Marshal, we have real examples of the same usage. Ende meant even, *a lot, an aggregate number*, as Graff. ibid. Sax. Chron. p. 319, line 14. As in Latin Finis, Fines have two separate senses, so Ende. Nor can I doubt, but that as Ensis comes from Φερειν, †fendere, so Ende is the very same word as Finis, Fines.

FARLAC, *fear*, fol. 44. a. 17. Godlec, fol. 48. a. 10. The termination -lac appears oftener now than in earlier times. See the Ormulum, vol. ii. p. 649, also Mennissclegge, Modeglegge. I find Schendlac, The Wooing of our Lord, fol. 130. d.: Wedlac, see this glossary. Mekelec, Hali Meidenhad, fol. 126. a. Brudlac, ib. fol. 127. a. Hendelac, ib. fol. 129. c. Scinlac, *fantasma*, Herbarium, lx. Woulecke, *wooing*, Ancren Riwle, fol. 23. b. Replac, id. fol. 49. a.

FIKEN, *to deceive.* fol. 47. b. 20. Fikelen, *to deceive,* Fikelung, *deception*, Wiheles, *deceits*, Wiles, Guiles, fol. 47. b. 7. Oreisun of Seinte Marie, fol. 70. b. 7. St. Cath. v. 130. Ancren Riwle, fol. 19. b, fol. 20. a, fol. 20. b, fol. 21. a. The Saxon English had Ficcan, *to deceive*, Wið glegmenn we ficcað. De Officiis, fol. 104. line 8. A sibilate form was the common word Swican, *to deceive*. The Frisians had Fiecheln, *to flatter, to give good words*. Cf. Heucheln.

FLEOTAN, *to float,* 2. *to swim.* fol. 44. b. 7. What letteð þene fisc ? te uleoten to þan oðere. Layamon, 22009.

FLUTTEN, *to subsist*, Fluttung, *subsistence*. fol. 55. b. 15. Hali Meidenhad, fol. 120. a. c. Translated *sufficere,* but that is to be understood as *suffici*, Ancren Riwle, fol. 53. a. Mete and cloð þat heo mei flutten bi. ib. fol. 119. b.

FREOLICH, *ladylike,* fol. 42. a. 3. MS. B. fol. 47. b. 15. Freolic folc cwen. Beowulf. 1275. Hire freliche bodi, St. Cath. Titus, fol. 142. b. Feir ant freolich o wlite (*vultus*) ant owestum. ib. fol. —. Vor godleic ant for ureoleic iȝerned of monie. Ancren Riwle, fol. 49 a. here a substantive *for goodness and ladyhood yearned of many*. þurh þine freoliche fet. Wooing of our Lord, fol. 131. d. *lordly feet* : from ffea, *lord,* ffeo, *lady.* We had Froes as late as Drayton (Polyolbion, VIII.). Freoliche iwapned, *lordly.* Layamon, 28941.

GENEOW, *yawn*, fol. 44. a. 12, or perhaps *jaw*. The words Chin, Γενειον and the rest of that group are related to Yawn with all that stand round it.

GRA, *grey one,* an adjective taken substantively, fol. 41. b. 19, fol. 44. a. 15, fol. 46. a. 20. Used here as an expression of horror, with allusion to the gray wolf, perhaps. The Islandic Grár is translated also *malignus* by B. H.

HALEWI, *balsam,* fol. 48. a. 16. Kumeð ðerof smel of aromaz : oðer of swote healewi. Ancren Riwle. MS. Nero. A. xiv. fol. 74. b. is Kumeð þer smel of aromaz : oðer of swote basme ? MS. Cleop. C. vi. fol. 123. b. in the Titus MS. a folio is missing between 68 and 69. The interpretation *balsam* assigned to the word in Layamon by the editor is therefore well supported. So, þu attrest þe wið halewi. ant wundest þe wið salue. ib. fol. 76. a.=127. a. It is spoken of as a drink, Ancren Riwle, fol. 63. b. as ismecched,

GLOSSARY. 103

ysmacked, tasted, fol. 22. b. 20. St. Cath. fol. 28. b. But our passage as above, and this, Schoteð niht ant dai hise earewen idrencte of an atter haliwei toward tin heorte to wundi þe wið. (Hali Meidenhad, fol. 116. b.) bring us to an *unguent* with which arrows are poisoned. We shall therefore reject the explanations of the word as *holy whey, holy cup,* and prefer the Mœsogothic 𐌰𐌻𐌴𐍅, *oil.*

HATEL, *keen,* fol. 55. a. 9. See Heteueste. Lo ich holde her hetel sweord ouer þin heaued. Ancren Riwle, fol. 110. b.

HATTERLICH, *persecuting.* fol. 38. b. 7. where R. uses it as a substantive, if the reading be not of a mistake. Cf. Ƿehtan, Ehtan, Peteube. Beowulf, 3649. William and the Werwolf, fol. 13. Hatter, *to harass, to fret.* Bakers Northamptonshire Glossary.

HETEUESTE, *sharply fast, bitingly fast.* fol. 45. b. 3. Hetelice, *mordicus.* Ælfric Gram. p. 42. Heteliche ðurhðyde. Homilies, vol. i. p. 452. *keenly thrust him through.* Hetelice slogon. Chronicle, p. 338, line 4. Bunden hire þerto harde ant hetefeste. Juliana, fol. 66. a. 9. Ancren Riwle, fol. 65. a, fol. 83. a. Hu ha þe bunden swa hetelifaste þat te blod wrang ut. Wooing of our Lord, fol. 131. b. *so that the blood squeezed out.* The adverb, St. M. fol. 42. a. 1. If Hetelice means *mordicus,* Hete may mean *a gnawing,* and explain Layamon, 20442, 20728.

HOFLES, *unsatisfactory,* fol. 51. a. 3. Cf. Saxon English Ƿof, *acceptable, agreeable.* Laws of Alfred, xliii. Danish Hove, *to like, to fancy, to please.* Puncheð hofles ant hoker. Hali Meidenhad, fol. 125. b. Nydbehoflic, *necessarius,* Beda, p. 618. 3. Ancren Riwle, fol. 26. b, where the editor cites an equivalent Latin MS. having *ridiculum.* Hoefwa, *quod alicui convenit.* Ohoefwelig, *indecorus.* (Ihre.) This root word forms Behove, Behoof, German Behuf, Friesic Bihof.

IWURÐEN, *become together,* fol. 48. a. 9. Elsewhere I have shewn (Spoon and Sparrow, 261.) that the Mœsogothic Ga, the Saxon English Ge, etc. are identical with the Latin Con, which in Κοινός is also visible unaltered in the Hellenic. Hence it is that χepeopðan means *convenire, agree*; its elements are *become* and *together.*

†LÆCAN, here Luken, *to tear,* præt. Leac, past part. Locen, Luken: fol. 41. a. 22, fol. 41. b. 6. 16, fol. 42. a. 21. etc. See Alocen, Tolocen, in Lye and Manning. Ichulle leoten (*make*) deor (θηρία) toteoren aut toluken þe. Juliana, fol. 58. a. 7. Toloken limel. ib. 14. *limb meal.* þat istelet irn: tolimede hire ant teleac lið ba ant

lire. ib. fol. 66. a. 13 *that steely iron limbed her and leac limb both and leor (complexion)*. As wilde deor to luken ham. fol. 70. a. 2. Lete to luken þi flesch þe fuheles of þe lufte. St. Cath. 2123. Layamon, 24843, 2603.

LÆCAN, *go*, præt. Lahte, fol. 44. a. 6. 8. þa hit winter læhte. Sax. Chron. p. 256, line 15, ed. 1861 : when the translator put *drew nigh*, he was thinking of neahlæhte, disowning the simple verb when it was before his eyes.

LAKE, *a wet place*, fol. 48. b. 2. On halgan weies lake. Cod. dipl. ccclxi. Low German Lake, *puddle, swamp*. Cf. Lega, *die Tiefe. Niedrigung* (Wiarda). Lacha, *palus*, Graff. vol. ii. col. 100. Kemble (cod. dipl. vol. III. xxxiii.) puts it down as Lacu feminine, but it may be often read neuter, ðat lake. He observes, "a smaller collection of water bore that name among the Saxons than we appropriate the name to." The words above I interpret *of the holy way*, meaning *full of holes*.

LANHURE, *at once*, fol. 46. b. 18, fol. 47. a. 21. It has escaped the notice of several, who have attacked this word, that it is the Saxon English Lanȝpe, Lunȝpe, first given by Benson, as *statim*. The sense seems to require *instantly* in Beowulf, 3253. Cædmon, p. 148. 24. Judith, line 147, ed. Grein. In Beowulf 1851, 4321, Kemble is content with this sense, *confestim, illico*. Nor is there anything against it. In Chronicle, anno 1065, p. 334. foot, *suddenly* is sufficient. In the former passage from St. Marh. the sense tentatively assigned to Lanhure, namely *at least, at all events*, is not apt. To pretend a derivation from La, An, Huru is so clumsy scholar craft that the devils of these tales must laugh and dance to read it. The unhappy wight who has swallowed it will burst "amid hips." Ich mihte inoh raðe wel habben awealt hire ȝif ha nalde wið luue wið luðer eie lanhure. St. Cath. 557. *I might quick enough have wielded* (or *controlled*) *her, if she ne would with love with evil awe at once*. Ȝif me is leved þurh mi leve lauerd for to leggen ham adun þat tu þi misbileaue lete þenne lanhure ant lihte to me. Ib. 771. *If leave is given me through my dear lord to lay them down, that thou let then at once thy misbelief and a-light to me.* And ȝif þu nult nanes weis witen þat he wrahte þulliche wundres lef lanhure þat tu sest. Ib. 1074. *And if thou ne wilt no wise wit that he wrought the like wonders, believe at once what thou seest.* Hefde he lanhure him scluen alesed. Ib. 1149. *Had he at once released himself.* Nu þeonne bisecbe ich þe uor þe luue þet ich kuðe þe þet tu luuie me lanhure. Ancren Riwle, MS. Cleop. fol. 107. b. *Now then I beseech thee for the love that I shewed thee, that thou love me at once.* I take it that the Latin *saltem* interprets the other reading, hure ant hure. In our fol. 46. b. 18. *at least* is impossible. þɘ iweddede þonken him þat ha lanhure hwen ha alles walden fallen duneward ;' ne fellen nawt. Hali Meidenhad, fol. 117. d. *The y-wedded thank God that they, when they altogether willed to fall downward, fell not at once.* He greiðede ham lanhure þa ha walden of meidenes hehschipe. a swuch stude. Ib. fol. 118. b. *He prepared them at once, when they would have of maidens highship, such a stead.* So Ib. fol. 119. b.

LEINEN, *lins, pools,* fol. 48. b. 1. So me (*men*) deoppre wadeð into ðe ueondes (*fiends*) leienenne ;' so me (*man*) kumeð later up. Ancren Riwle, fol. 89. b. Hwase lið ileinnen deope bisunken. Hali Meidenhad, fol. 121. d. *Whosoever lieth in lins deep sunken.*

LIÐEREN, *to lather,* fol. 40. b. 21. of the weak conjugation. Cf. Lödur, *spuma* (Wormius, Lex. Run. p. 75). Loeddr, *spuma aquæ saponatæ* (Ihre); ȝeleþþeð, *lathered,* Lib. Med. i. 4. Beten hire swa luðere þat hire leofliche lich liðeri al oblote. Juliana, fol. 58. a. 21. Similarly St. Cath. fol. 27. a. Layamon, 7489.

MAN, fol. 48. a. 3. for Geman see art. 19. The sense *concubitus* decorously hidden under this term may be sufficiently seen in Lyes quotations for Gemana. ȝeornliche to witen hu ha mahte best witen hire unwemmet ant hire meiðhad wiðuten man of monne. Juliana, fol. 57. a. 4. *Anxiously to know how she might best preserve herself unpolluted and her maidenhood without commerce with man.* Nam of hire flesch wiðuten meane of wepmon. (MSS. Cott. Titus, D. xviii. fol. 129. b.) *Christ took of Mary flesh without commerce of male.* Wiarda in his Altfriesisches Wörterbuch attributes to Monna the sense "Sich fleischlich vermischen," but has not supported his statement by examples. Manda the subst. as "fleischliche Vermischung" occurs in the laws of West Friesland (p. 433. 25. ed. R.). "Hwerso een man ende een frowe duaet togara cleppen, iefta dio frowe spreckt dat hio see mit ene kinda, ioff di man biseckt dis manda, so ontgonge hi mit siner seluer sexter hand, etc." *Wherever a man and a frow do clip together, in case the frow saith that she be with child, if the man denies the concubitus, then let him get off by swearing himself clear along with his father, mother, sister,*

P

brother, child and grandchild. And in a document of A.D. 1404 (p. 485. ed. R.) Iefter en man deer hat een æfta frouwa, ende een frouwa deer hath een æften man, ende letet ayder hiara æfte zyd sitta, ende werpeth hiara manda togære ende hiare menscip. *If a man has a lawful frow and a frow has a lawful husband, and each of them lets the lawful consort be, and they put toqether their concubitus and their consorting.* Monda answers to the German Gemeinde: of the accretionary D see Spoon and Sparrow, 468.

ME, *but.* See Remarks on the Language, page 77, art. 9.

MELSEOCEL, *honeysuckle,* fol. 46. a. 13. This hibrid word is paralleled by Meledeaw, *honey dew,* in Codex Exon. which is our Mildew, now applied to smut in wheat, and mouldiness in eatables, for the butcher will say the meat is mildewed. Melseotel was printed because it looks more like that in the original.

NEBSCHAFT, *nebship, neb, face,* fol. 40. a. 2. Juliana, fol. 65. a. 21. Face is a Latinism, and the Saxon English Neb with this word were used in the most serious way. Ʒe schulen habben þer uppe ðe brihte sihte of Godes nebscheft. Ancren Riwle, fol. 22. b. 24. *Ye shall have the bright sight of Gods nebship.* Godes brihte nebscheft. Ib. fol. 43. b.

NEODELUKEST, *very closely, studiosissime,* fol. 48. a. 2. Beda, p. 516. 4. For the source of the signification Spoon and Sparrow, art. 605.

NOðELATERE, *nevertheless, none the less,* fol. 51. b. 12. Ancren Riwle, fol. 92. b.

NOWCIN, *harm, hurt,* fol. 37. b. 9, fol. 45. a. 1. St. Cath. fol. 28. b, fol. 30. a, fol. 36. a. Till better information we may take this as Noþ-cun, *need-kin, kind of compulsion,* by exchange of Wen and þorn, not from Nocere, on account of the long vowel and termination.

NURð, *murmuring, lamenting cry,* fol. 54. b. 7. Hare nurð ant hare untohe bere. Si sciret, fol. 1. b. 4. *Their nurð and their untoward noise.* Nyarr, Nyarb, *to fret, to be discontented,* Jamieson.

OUERGAT, OUERGART, *pride, presumption,* fol. 45. a. 5, fol. 50. a. 13. The R is inserted as in Harland in Gawin Douglas for Halend, our Haling, Hawling; in the Ancren Riwle, Iturpled for Toppled. Forgart occurs in the Ormulum, and I do not accept the editors account of the word. Our Get, the older ȝitan, was applied to the faculties of the mind as in Anðȝit, and that root we have here.

GLOSSARY. 107

Reh, *fierce*, fol. 47. b. 11. hɼeoh. See Layamon, vol. iii. 4062.
Even such passages as 18709 must be thus translated, *trux, truculentus*. Perhaps as Τραχυς to Rough, so Trux to Reh.

Ro, *rest, quiet*, fol. 53. a. 19. ɼoρe, dative, Cod. Ex. p. 115. 4. fem. Ro, Danish, Swedish; Ruhe, *rest*, German. Rawa, ohg. fem. Ro, Ormulum, Political Songs, p. 149.

Rondin, *rend*, fol. 42. a. 3, is I believe only another form of Rendin. Otherwise the word should mean *Rod, strike with Rod*; Rod=Round=Rung=Mœsogothic Hrugga, ῥάβδος: the first three are equivalents in Old English. We seem to have such a word in the unexplained Radrond of the Emsiger Busstaxen. " Fotsporne achta pannigar. Stefsleck achte pannegar. Delefal achte pannegar. Blotlesa achte pannegar. Radrond achte pannigar." p. 212. *A spurn with the foot eight pennies. A staff blow eight pennies. A downfall eight pennies. Blood fetched eight pennies. A rod-round eight pennies.*

Ruglinge, *sprawlingly on the back*, fol. 51. a. 22. Rugghelinck, *supinus, resupinus*. Kilian. Ryglangs, *backwards*, Danish. To interpret Wrigglingly would be wrong, for in 1200 A.D. the W was pronounced.

Si, *victory*, fol. 56. a. 7. Siȝe, Siȝe in Layamon. German Siege.

Sihen here *ascend*, præt. Sah, past part. Sihen, fol. 55. b. 3. Ant te edle engles wið hire sawle singinde sihen toward heouene. Juliana, fol. 69. b. 10. Siȝan must therefore have the same sense: thus also Stiȝan is usually *ascend*, but sometimes descend : perhaps they are no more originally than Step, Στειχειν. St. Cath. 2353, 2084.

Smeat, *tried, tested*, fol. 46. a. 14, from, as I suppose, Smeagan: not *smithied*.

Snarchen, *to frizzle*, præt. Schnarchte, fol. 51. b. 21, in Osnaburgh Snerken, in low German Snirren. (Bremisch Wörterbuch.) Compare Snerple, *to shrivel up by means of fire*.

Sprechi, *I strike off a spark*, fol. 49. b. 7. The verb is related to the substantive, and to Spring, when said of planks, to Spray of waves and of trees, to Spreathed hands, and to several old words still known in our woodlands and moors. Swedish Spricka, *to spring, to split, to spreathe, to burst*. Spräcka, *to break*, Spränga, *to split*, etc. etc. etc. It is found probably in the Paris Psalter, Ps. ci. 3. Forðon dagas mine | gedroren syndan | smece gelice, | and for-

p 2

spyrcende synd | mine mearh cofan, | þæs þe me þinceð, | swylce hi on cocer pannan | cocas gehyrstan. *Thence my days are gone like smoke and my marrow coves (or bones) are sputtering sparks as seemeth to me, as if in cooking pans cooks were frying them.*

SPUTTE, *enticed*, fol. 48. a. 18; pres. Sput. þenne spit leccherie to schome. Hali Meidenhad, fol. 117. a. þet flesch sput propremen toward swetnesse ant toward eise ant toward softnesse. Ancren Riwle. Cleop. fol.... I suspect Sput to be the third sing. pres. of Spanan, *entice*, by rejection of N, and Sputte to be an altered weak form (Language, art. 49) for Speon, *enticed*.

STEAP, *bright, brilliant, fiery, burning*, fol. 44. a. 2, fol. 48. a. 17. Compare Steem, *a lowe of fyre*, Prompt. Parv. Stew, Stove and so forth, the original idea of which is that of warmth. On hise mouth it stod a stem, Als it were a sunne beam. Havelok, 590, with So stod ut of his mouth a glem Rith al swilk so the sunne beam, 2122, and with the French. Compare also Stived, *baked hard*, William and Werwolf, fol. 44. b. In Sanskrit Sp͟ūmah, *light, lustre*, Wilsons Lex. Perhaps the root reappears without sibilation in Θύειν, Thus, *incense*, Θυμός, *anger*. Since the Saxon English for frankincense was Ster, the language used Thus, Thuris with sibilation: as also Στύραξ which is compared by Marshall. (Gospels, p. 539.) Steam seems to be a participial derivative. The sense above should be assigned to the word in the following passages. Steapne hrof, Beowulf, 1846, *the brilliant roof*; Steapne rond, 5125, *the brilliant shield*; Heaðo steapa helm, *the brilliant helmet*, 2483, 4299, 6298. As applied to a helmet, however, we must remember the remark of Wiarda on the Asegabuch, p. 293. The text is Ac skilu wi use lond wera mith egge and mith orde. and mith tha brune. [skelde?] with thene stapa helm. and with thene rada skeld. p. 273. We must guard our land with edge and with point, and with the brown shield [the brynie?] with the steap helm and with the red, [brada, broad?] shield. Wiarda says that a parallel text has Hoge, *high*. Steap, *bright*, is a natural epithet for eyes. He is blæcfexede and cyrps hwit on lichaman and he hæfð steape eagan. Homilies, vol. i. p. 456. *he has bright eyes.* þe keiser bisturede hire wið. swiðe steape ehnen. St. Cath. line 309. *The kaiser stared at her with very fiery eyes.* Schinende and schenre þen eni ʒimstanes steapre þen is steorre. Id. 2661. *Shining and sheener than any gemstones, brighter than is a star.* His eyen stepe and rolling in his hed. Chaucer, C. T. Prolog. l. 201. Princes and warriors in their armour are also bright, brilliant, and in this way the word often occurs in Layamon, as heretoȝe steapne, 5879. This inductive reasoning wants the support of some old gloss, which I have not as yet found.

STEORCNAKET, may be read Steortnaket as in low German, for the letters C and T are not distinguishable in this MS. Juliana, fol. 58. b. 20, fol. 60. b. 3. The language may have also contained both forms, as in ꝼoꝛꞅꝓoꝯcen, Matth. xxiv. 19, compared with Swart. But while the question was open to doubt it seemed better to adhere to the more familiar. The old Friesic was Stoknaked, which is of intelligible elements.

STEORUE, *fierce of face*, fol. 46. b. 17, fol. 50. a. 22. An equivalent with sibilation of the Latin Torvus. Storvigh, *Torvus*. Kilian.

STEW, *restrain*, fol. 41. a. 16, fol. 50. a. 22. Stew þe storue of helle. Juliana, fol. 64. a. 17. Stew swuchhe wordes, fol. 59. b. 18. St. Cath. 373. Stute þu þenne ant stew | þe ant stille þine wordes. ib. 1540. =fol. 27. a. istewet ant stille. ib. 657. Stoewen, *compescere, coercere*. (Kilian.)

STRICEN, *to run*, præt. Strac, plur. Striken, fol. 41. a. 11, fol. 45. b. 16, fol. 51. b. 2. Comen alle strikinde strengest te swiðest of eauer euch strete. St. Cath. R. fol. 18. b. Ant strikeð a stream ut of þat stanene þurh þat ha in resteð. St. Cath. 2514. 733. In the metrical paraphrase of Boethius, p. 177, the verb is used of the revolution of the sky about the earth. In the Ormulum, of the march into the Red Sea. Perhaps its frequentative with loss of sibilation is Trickle. Isl. Strik is interpreted *cursus directus*. Layamon, 27475, 27589, makes the præterite Stræhte.

STUDGE, *go staggeringly*, fol. 44. b. 12. Ne studgi ȝe neauer. Juliana, fol. b. 11. *hesitate*. St. Cath. fol. 24. a. " Studging, *walking with short heavy steps*; always used with the adjunct along; He goes studging along; often applied to old agricultural labourers." Bakers Northants Gloss. Cf. with frequentative R, Stagger: also Στειχειν.

STUTEN, *to stop*, fol. 41. a. 16, fol. 44. b. 11. Ha stutte, *she ceased*, Juliana, fol. 67. b. 3. þat tear he astutte. St. Cath. 23. *there he stopped.* Anone to the forest they found (*went*). There they stotede a stound (*time*). Sir Degrevant, 225. One is said to stoit, when he hits his Foot against a Stone or moves like one drunk. Glossary to Allan Ramsays poems. Ga-Stoþanan in the Mœsogothic is στῆσαι actively. Rom. xiv. 4. The frequentative seems to be Stutter, *stop often*.

SULLICH, *rare*, fol. 51. a. 11. ɼelb-lıc, ɼellıc, ɼẏllıc. Ha hine þis word sulliche sende. Juliana, fol. 57. b. 10. His sulliche sune. fol. 65. b. 6. Ælf. Homil. vol. ii. p. 466. Layamon, vol. i. p. 274= 6428.

SWINDEN, *make to disappear*, fol. 45. a. 14, a verb usually neuter.

TAUELIN, *talk*, fol. 48. a. 9. Nefde hare nan tunge to tauelin a dint. St. Cath. fol. 24. a. Bitauelet. St. Cath. fol. 24. b. Tauelin in St. Cath. Reg. 19. 8.=Talien, Titus, 138. a. Nu we schulen talien. take ut of his tunge and tauele wið me. St. Cath. fol. 19. b. In low German, Tauelen=Tauelken is *to speak slow, to drawl*.

TEKEN, *to eke*, fol. 40. a. 16. So Ancren Riwle, fol. 26. b, fol. 36. a, fol. 40. a. ult., fol. 43. b, fol. 45. a, fol. 65. a. Hali Meidenhad, fol. 121. b, fol. 123. a. Wooing of our Lord, fol. 132. d.

TOGGEN, *to toy*, fol. 48. a. 19. Mid wouhinge mid togginge. Ancren Riwle, fol. 53. b. *with wooing, with toying*. The same word as Tug, *pull* : in old Friesic laws Toga is used of the pulling about a woman rudely.

TOLLEN, *to fondle with the hand*, præt. Tulde. fol. 48. a. 19. Cf. Tallazjan, *palpare*, Tollon, *plaudere, to pat* (horses necks), Graff. vol. v. col. 397. More loosely *to coax* ; Of tollinde lokunges. Ancren Riwle, fol. 11. b. *of coaxing lookings*. Ame dogge ga herut hwet wult þu nu herinne. þis tolleð him inwart. Ib. fol. 78. a. *Ah me, dog! go out. What wilt thou now in here? This coaxes him inward.* Sire. mi liht onswere. oðer mine lihte lates. tulden him earst upon me. Ancren Riwle, fol. 87. a. *Sir, my light answer or my light behaviour enticed him first upon me.* Mid wouhinge. mid togginge oðer mid eni tollunge ·/ mid gigge leihtre. mid hor eien mid eni lihte lates mid ȝeoue mid tollinde wordes oðer mid luue speche cos unhende gropunges þet beoð heaued sunnen. Ancren Riwle, fol. 53. b. *With wooing, with toying, or with any caressing, with giggling laughter, with horish eyes, with any light manners, with gift, with enticing words, or with love speech, kiss, indecorous gropings, which be head sins.* Ne makie ȝe none gistninges ·/ ne ne tulle ȝe to þe ȝete none unkuðe harloz. Ib. fol. 115. *Ne make ye no guestings ; nor entice ye to the gate no unknown varlets.* Vor nabbe ȝe nout þene nome. ne ne schulen habben þurh þe grace of Gode of totinde ancres ne of tollinde lokunges ne lates.

Ib. fol. 11. b. *For ye have not the name, nor shall have, through the grace of God, of peeping anchorites nor of coaxing lookings nor manners.* þis is wowunge efter godes grome ant tollunge of his vuel. Ib. fol. 29. *Wooing of Gods wrath and inviting of his evil.*

> Stay thy harpe, thou proud harper,
> For Gods love I pray thee,
> For and thou playes as thou beginns
> Thou'lt till my bryde from mee.
> King Estmere, 229, in Percys Rel.

I am willing to believe that þukl, n. *contrectatio*, at þukla, *palpare, contrectare* in Biörn Haldorsen are earlier forms, before assimilation, and related to Touch, Θιγεῖν, with L frequentative.

UNGEINLICHE, fol. 44. a. 12. Gain is *commodum*, Ungainly is *incommode*, Gein spoken of roads is only *compendiosus* as that is *commodus*: ʒein, *commodus*, occurs in the Epistola Alexandri: *commodum*, St. Marh. here fol. 51. b. 9. The root syllable seems to approach the earlier forms of Unne, below.

UNNAN, *to favour*, fol. 54. b. 8. The sense *concedere* passes to *favere*. The substantive Unne is *favour* in Laws and Inst. p. 115, line 40. The cognates are the Norse Unna, the reciprocal form of which Unnask, is *to entertain mutual affection*; þan Helgi ok Sváva veittusk varar ok unnusk furðu mikit. Helgakviða Hiorv. S. 31. in Sæmunds prose; *Helgi and Svava exchanged troth and loved each other wondrous mickle*; the German Gönnen, *to permit*, Gunst, *leave, favour*, the low German Gunnen, of old written also Gannen, where they alledge an ancient gloss, Gegant, Gegunnet, *favore addictum*, the Mœsogothic Ansts, χάρις, and the Latin Venia, which is as large in its range as any of its northern kindred. Speaking of this coincidence to a learned friend, he immediately added חֵן, *gratia, favor, benevolentia*, חַנָּה, *Hannah*, יְהוֹחָנָן, and חָנַן, *favit*. God, *good*, in the passage above is used adverbially as in God likeþ, fol. 53. a. 20. Cf. yfeles unnon. Paris Psalter, Ps. xxxix. 17.

UNOFSERUET, *undeserved*, fol. 50. b. 5. þu hauest for me swa muche iwraht wiðuten min ofseruinge. Juliana, fol. 67. a. 19. Cf. Ancren Riwle, fol. 62. b, fol. 63. a.

WANDRIEN, *to be in misery*, fol. 46. a. 11. Hwen hit þer to cumeð þat sar sorhfule angoise. þat stronge ant stikinke stiche þat unrotes uuel þat pine upo pine. þat wondrende ȝeomerunge. Hali Meidenhad, fol. 123. a. *When it comes to that, the sore sorrowful anguish, the strong and sticking stitch, the evil of disquiet, the pain upon pain, the miserable yammering.*

WANDREÐE, *mischief, danger, peril,* fol. 40. a. 9. Juliana, fol. 60. a. 5, fol. 60. b. 9, fol. 61. a. 4, fol. 62. b. 13. Si sciret, fol. 4. b. 5. Hali Meidenhad, fol. 114. b. St. Cath. Titus, fol. 137. b. Ancren Riwle, fol. 99. b. Ormulum. Islandic, Vandræði. Hann kom Asum jafnan í fullt vandræði. Snorra Edda, p. 18. Wandráde, *discrimen, difficultas*. Ihre. In þis lyf ful of wandreþ | of pyne, baret, and unleþ. MSS. Additional, 22283, fol. 7. b.

WASTUM, *growth,* fol. 38. b. 7. See notes on Orientis Mirabilia, XXII. Layamon, 15699.

WEDLAC, *wedlock,* Iweddet, fol. 40. b. 4, fol. 37. b. 19. For the termination see Fearlac. Wed, the Latin Vas, Vadem, *a pledge,* was properly applied to espousal, betrothal; and it is so used in the Saxon English gospels, Matth. ii. 16 ; Beda, p. 529. 17. etc. To marry was Æwnian; the two are contrasted Chron. p. 314, line 37. But as the older word passed out of use, Wedlac came in. Wifian was *to have to do with women,* and is, under a sibilate form, Chaucers Swive. These matters have been lately discussed without the necessary knowledge. The Latin here has *accipiam te in coniugium,* MS. Harl. 5327. Quod accipiam te coniugem. MS. Harl. 2801.

-WILE is a termination of nearly the same sense as -ful: so Wrechwile, Hali Meidenhad, fol. 126. a.; Spatewile, Marh. fol. 47. a. 10; Hercwile, Ancren Riwle, fol. 24. b. 6.

WUMME, *alas,* fol. 47. b. 21. The signification is ascertained by, Nis ter na steuene bituhe þe fordemde. bute wumme ant wa is me ant wa beo þe. Si sciret, fol. 4. b. 10. *There ne is no steuene* (†σφωνη, φωνη, sonus, *voice*) *between the for-doomed but Wumme!* and Wo *is me!* and Wo *be thee!* Sohte þe te seonne wumme þat sihðe. Juliana, fol. 63. b. 18. *Sought thee to see, woe is me that sight.* Wumme wo is me. Ancren Riwle, fol. 41. a: so Titus, fol. 43. a. Cleopatra, fol. 65. b: the printed text is false. See the MS. B. reading of our present text, fol. 50. a. 5. Wæ in the earlier language is constructed with a dative, as pæ ðæm in Prol. IV. Euang. Lindisf. Gospels; whence Wumme=wæ me, probably. Compare Well is thee! Psalm cxxviii. 2. Liturgy.

GLOSSARY.

Wundre, *mischief, hurt*, fol. 48. b. 17. Compare Wandreðe. In this, Monie weneð wel to don þat deð al to wunder, St. Cath. MS. Cleop. C. vi. fol. 28. a, we find Deð al to cweade, that is, *bad*, in MS. Nero A. xiv. fol. 17. a. The word occurs Cleop. fol. 157. b= Nero, fol. 94. b. To schome and wundren. (Wooing of our Lord, fol. 131. d.) Tukeð ham al to wundre. Ancren Riwle, fol. 104. b, fol. 107. b. In the nearly cotemporary text of the Chronicle anno 1137, p. 882, line 16, Diden hi alle wunder; in the translation no confidence should be placed.

Wurðung, *mire, dung*, fol. 39. a. 5. They did take and carry certain worthing or dung from the said monastery, and bestowed it on their own farm holds. Whitakers Richmondshire, vol. ii. p. 382. Bi hwam hit is iwriten þus þurh þe prophete þat ha in hare wurðunge as eaueres forroteden. þat is eauereuch wif þat is hire were þral and liueð iwurðinge he ant heo baðe. Ah nis hit nawt bi þeose iseid þat ha forrotieð þrin ʒif ha hare wedlac laheliche halden. Ah þa ilke sari wrecches þat iþat ilke fule wurðinge unweddede walewið:' beoð þe deueles eaueres þat rit ham ant spureð ham to don al þat he will. þeos waleweð in wurðinge ant forroteð þrin. Hali Meidenhad, fol. 116. a. *Of whom it is y-written thus by the prophet, that they in their mire as boars rotted away. That is every woman that is her mans thrall and liveth in mire he and she both. But it is not of these y-said that they rot away therein if they hold lawfully their wedlock. But the same sorry wretches that in the same foul mire unwedded wallow, etc.*

ʒeien, *to cry*, præt. ʒeide, fol. 55. a. 19. 14. Juliana, 67. b. 3. Ha ʒeide to godd. fol. 66. a. 19. We ʒeieð upon him ofte. Ancren Riwle, fol. 18. Heo mei longe ʒeien er God hire ihere. ibid. We ʒeieð to him iðe paternoster. ib. fol. 31. b. Also fol. 36. b, fol. 38. b, fol. 39. a, fol. 61. b, fol. 71. a, fol. 78. a. 18. Cf. Islandic at geya, *to bark*.

ʒuren, *to chatter*, præt. ʒurde. fol. 50. a. 3. Wið þat:' þe unwiht ʒurde þat monie weren awundret hwat te ʒuring mahte beon. Juliana, fol. 64. b. 9. Bigon to beaten þen belial of helle. ant he to rarin reowliche ant to ʒuren ant te ʒeien. Juliana, fol. 64. a. 9. ʒeinde ant ʒurende. St. Cath. 161: so 2040. The radix, which is that also of Chirp, Chirm, Cry, Greet and Garrire, is found in ʒeor. Ancren Riwle, fol. 83. a.=ʒur in Titus, fol. 76. a.

THE END.

Add to art. 42, page 91.

Hwonne is used in a relative sense in the poetical life of St. Guðlac, Cod. Ex. p. 108. line 34, p. 116. line 16, p. 148. line 28. Hwan. Chron. p. 367. line 10, p. 369. line 25, p. 371. line 33.

Add to page 50, line 14.

" Who shall doubt, Donne, wher I a poet be ? "
Ben Jonson, Epigr. xcvi.

Add to page 105, line 27.

Mána, in the poetical Juliana, (Cod. Ex. p. 244. line 20.) might be intended by the poet in the sense of ʒemanena, συνουσιῶν ; the genitival -ena would collapse into -a (art. 30) ; cf. Leoma, *of eyes*, for leomena. Cod. Ex. p. 353. line 6.

Printed by Taylor and Francis, Red Lion Court, Fleet Street.

www.ingramcontent.com/pod-product-compliance
Lightning Source LLC
Chambersburg PA
CBHW031347160426
43196CB00007B/761